Indian Business Case Studies

Indian Business Case Studies

Volume V

ROOPA PRAVEEN

DILIP AHER

NILESH ANUTE

Indian Case Studies in Business Management

OXFORD
UNIVERSITY PRESS

OXFORD
UNIVERSITY PRESS

Great Clarendon Street, Oxford, ox2 6dp,
United Kingdom

Oxford University Press is a department of the University of Oxford.
It furthers the University's objective of excellence in research, scholarship,
and education by publishing worldwide. Oxford is a registered trade mark of
Oxford University Press in the UK and in certain other countries

© ASM Group of Institutes, Pune, India 2022

The moral rights of the authors have been asserted

First Edition published in 2022

Impression: 1

Published in the United States of America by Oxford University Press
198 Madison Avenue, New York, NY 10016, United States of America

British Library Cataloguing in Publication Data

Data available

Library of Congress Control Number: 2022938091

ISBN 978-0-19-286941-8

DOI: 10.1093/oso/9780192869418.001.0001

Printed in India by
Rakmo Press Pvt. Ltd.

Dr R.R. Pachpande
[1947–2009]

'Education is the Soul of our society'

*The series editors and the volume authors of the case volumes titled as
'Indian Business Case Studies' published by Oxford University Press have
a deep sense of gratefulness while dedicating these case volumes to the
memory of Dr Raghunath R. Pachpande, the Founder of ASM Group of
Institutes Pune, India.*

*It was with the untiring efforts and strategic vision of Dr R.R. (as he was
known to his close friends and colleagues) which has been instrumental in
ASM group adopting case methodology as a unique element in its pedagogy
which motivated the faculty and students of ASM group of institutes to
develop business case studies on Indian businesses and use them to teach
management subjects in all branches of business management studies.*

*Dr R.R. Pachpande was a leader beyond parlance and ahead of time in
establishing educational institutes more so in higher studies in business
management specifically in the industrial belts in the state of Maharashtra
with a view to providing best of experiential learning to its students
through closer interactions with business Units around.*

Today ASM Group continues the great legacy of Dr R.R. Pachpande under the leadership of his successors and who have succeeded in taking ASM Group to global recognition as a unique group of institutes offering world-class education in all branches of business management.

This case volume is dedicated to the memories of late Dr R.R. Pachpande.

Contents

SECTION II   CASE STUDIES IN
FINANCE MANAGEMENT

Preface

Many universities and management institutes across the globe have adopted the case study methodology for teaching almost all branches of management studies for several decades. This trend has been seen in India also, wherein the IIMs and progressive management institutes in private sector have implemented case methodology as an important pedagogical tool in business management education.

However, there is a severe shortage in Indian business case studies faced by the B-schools in India and those global institutes associated with Indian academia. Majority of the case studies studied at IIMs and other A-grade B-schools in India are from situations in industries in foreign countries and have very little or no relevance to Indian business situations. This acts as a major gap for faculty and students engagement in business management studies both at UG and masters level (PG) studies, wherein for clarification of theoretical concepts is possible mainly through use of case methodology which enables insight into business real-life business situations.

Besides, the objectives and purposes for which case studies are developed abroad are much different from course of studies in Indian B-schools. Therefore, the dependence on foreign case studies for Indian students does not provide any real situational insight on Indian business. Although the curriculum requires taking the students through case study methodology, there are not many Indian case studies for this purpose.

The main objectives of using case-based teaching as a major pedagogical tool in B-schools are as follows:

1. To facilitate students' concept development capabilities through exposure to real-life problems in industries.
2. To enable students to correlate theoretical topics with the techniques used in analysing complex issues in business situations.

3. To develop skills using which students can develop application matrix for the theoretical topics for real-life problem analysis and resolution techniques.

4. Help the students of B-schools to develop orientation towards the important attributes and attitudinal requirements for effective handling of complex situations at the workplace.

5. To develop a clear understanding of the techniques used for problem analysis, situation analysis, and decision analysis and appropriate understanding of the difference between problems and situations in management.

6. To develop the group-based approaches to solving problems and challenges at the workplace by appropriate coordination of and collaboration with all related aspects of a situation.

7. To develop a reference manual for recording the problems tackled and the essential lessons learnt from past incidences for use in future eventualities of recurrence of issues

8. To develop the preventive steps that must be initiated to ensure the problems resolved once do not recur in the immediate future.

Business case studies are basically oriented towards developing the evaluative and analytical skills of students in industry situations. Such case studies draw the attention of participants of the case resolution methodology on the in-depth correlative evaluation of the issues in the case study with the various related topics that the students have to study about in their classrooms. These case studies could be on issues related to human resources, industrial relations, product and process, marketing and finance management areas in business management.

The academic environment across the world too is facing a major disruption on account the global pandemic COVID-19 forcing the offline education system to switch over to online/blended versions of teaching and learning process. And use of case methodology and simulation exercises are the main in gradients for sustaining effective ways of delivering experiential learning through the use of case and case lets in an online mode of teaching ensuring student engagements and online interactive ways of knowledge dissemination.

Oxford University Press in association with ASM Group of Institutes Pune, India is publishing for the first time comprehensive case volumes as series of eight volumes with case studies on Indian businesses selected from all aspects of business functions like HR, Finance Marketing, and Operations+ providing an exciting and long waited opportunity to faculty and students across the globe to access Indian Business Case Studies through these case volumes.

We are very confident that the case volumes will receive very good response and will be of utmost use to the readers.

Acknowledgements

The series editors wish to acknowledge with thanks the contribution of data for the case studies from ASM's Academic Associates the CETYS University Mexico—Dr Scott Venezia, Dean International Affairs and Dr Francisco Velez Dean of Colleges CETYS Mexico.

As also of several senior faculty from ASM Group of Institutes for their help in proofreading and editing of the case studies.

We also acknowledge the numerous news reporters of daily newspapers in business and economics in India which have been rich and authentic secondary data sources for design and development of case studies for the case volumes.

About the Series Editors

Dr Sandeep Pachpande, Chairman
ASM Group of Institutes, Pune, India

Prof J.A. Kulkarni, Professor,
ASM Group of Institutes, Pune, India

Both the series editors have decades of experience in business case design and development as also implementation of case methodology of teaching for the faculty and students of business schools in India and abroad.

The series editors have to their credit of authoring three major books on business case studies published by globally known publishers and in conducting workshops for case design and development.

The series editors have a very good network with leaders and stalwarts in Business Management studies across the globe and popular as keynote speakers in many national and international conferences. They have a very rich experience in organizing national and international conferences and case competitions.

Currently the series editors are busy completing a unique case analysis and resolution methodology program which is under copyright considerations.

Dr Sandeep Pachpande   Prof J.A. Kulkarni

About the Series Editors

Dr Sudeep Deshpande, Chairman
ASM Group of Institutes, Pune, India

Prof. A. Kulkarni, Professor
ASM Group of Institutes, Pune, India

About the Volume Authors

Dr Roopa Praveen MCA, MCM PhD

Experience: Dr Roopa has a very broad experience background of more than 20years developing skill sets that draws on a rare and valuable mix of business, networking, customer service, marketing, programs management, education and technical projects reengineering business operations (both academic and industry oriented) for optimal results, and spanning operations optimization, performance assessment, cross-functional team leadership and collaborations, issue resolution, client management, regulatory compliance, and quality assurance.

Area of expertise

Business Development | Coaching & Development | Marketing | Strategic Planning & Execution | Team Management & Leadership | Revenue & Profit Improvement | Networking & Communication | Regulatory Compliance | Process & Efficiency Improvement | Risk Assessment& Management | Creative thinking | Organization Development | Innovative Strategic Planning

Publications

Dr Roopa Praveen has published more than 15 research papers in National and International Conferences. Has authored and edited several business case studies on Indian and international businesses and has contributed immensely in the adoption of case methodology as an important part of the institutional pedagogy.

Dr Dilip Aher—Associate Professor MBS (HR), MMS (Mkt), PhD
ASM, Institute of Business Management & Research,
Chinchwad, Pune

Experience: Total 31 years
Industry: 20 years as an Asst. Manager at Deepak Nitrite Ltd,
Academic: 11 years in ASM Group & Sinhgad Institute, Pune.

Research paper publications:
1. SCOPUS Listed: **02**
2. UGC CARE listed: **07**
3. International Journal: **06**
4. National journal: **03**
5. Certification Courses: **10**

Dr Nilesh Anute MA, MBA, Phd Associate Professor at ASM Group IBMR

- Subjects Taught:
  - Business Research Methods
  - Basics of Marketing
  - Marketing Management
  - Digital Marketing
  - Marketing Research

REWARDS & RECOGNITIONS
- Appreciated by The Best Faculty Award of ASM's Mindscape event 2018.
- Appreciated by The Best Teacher Award of NBN Sinhgad School of Management Studies in 2017.
- Appreciated by Young Scholars Inc as a mentor for Books 2 Biz Program in 2014.

CERTIFICATION COURSES (54) NPTEL Online Certification
- Leadership—Indian Institute of Technology, Kharagpur
- Consumer Psychology—Indian Institute of Technology, Guwahati
- Marketing Research and Analysis—Indian Institute of Technology, Roorkee
- English Language for Competitive Exams—Indian Institute of Technology, Madras

- Global Marketing Management—Indian Institute of Technology, Roorkee
- Google Scholar—Citation: 18, h index: 2, i10 index: 1

Publications

Authored and presented **35 Research Papers** in National and International Conferences and Workshops.

A Teaser for the Readers

Why focus on Indian Business Case Studies?

Business Case Studies on Indian Business Environment

The crux of the issues

Business Case Studies and their relevance to Management Education
Many B-schools outside India have adopted decades ago the case study methodology for teaching almost all branches of management studies. This trend has been seen in India also, wherein a majority of the Indian Institutes of Management (IIMs) have implemented case study-based methodology as an important pedagogical tool in business management education.

The major issue in India is, however, the inadequate interaction between B-schools and industries. The fault lies with both B-schools and the industry. The B-schools in a majority of cases cannot provide research-based solutions to industry problems due to a lack of necessary infrastructure and facilities. And the industries in the absence of any direct benefit from the institutes are not inclined to waste their time and funds on B-school education.

Hence, there is a severe shortage in Indian case studies through which the B-schools can provide industry insight to its students. Majority of the case studies studied at IIMs and other A-grade B-schools are imported from abroad. These case studies are from situations in industries in foreign countries and have very little or no relevance to Indian students who have to necessarily study the situations in Indian industries.

Besides, the objectives and purposes for which case studies are developed abroad are much different from the level and course of studies in Indian B-schools. Therefore, the dependence on foreign case studies for

Indian students does not provide any real situational insight on Indian business.

Although the syllabus for management studies requires taking the students through case study methodology, unfortunately there are not many Indian case studies that can be discussed with the students.

Thus, it is a Catch-22 situation. Unless institutes have the capability and the required infrastructure to cater to industry-related issues, they cannot expect any interactive support from the industries; unless institutes get adequate data from industries, their teaching content and quality continue to be much less than the expectations of the industry from students who pass out from such institutes.

This is not specific to Indian environment alone the same situation more or less is prevalent in most of the developed countries as well.

Objectives of Use of Case Study Methodology

The main objectives of using case-based teaching as a major pedagogical tool in B-schools are as follows:

1. To facilitate students' concept development capabilities through exposure to real-life problems in industries.
2. To enable students to correlate theoretical topics with the techniques used in analysing complex issues in business situations.
3. To develop skills using which students can develop application matrix for the theoretical topics for real-life problem analysis and resolution techniques.
4. Help the students of B-schools to develop orientation towards the important attributes and attitudinal requirements for effective handling of complex situations at the workplace.
5. To develop a clear understanding of the techniques used for problem analysis, situation analysis and decision analysis and appropriate understanding of the difference between problems and situations in management.
6. To develop the group-based approaches to solving problems and challenges at the workplace by appropriate coordination of and collaboration with all related aspects of a situation.

7. To develop a reference manual for recording the problems tackled and the essential lessons learnt from past incidences for use in future eventualities of recurrence of issues.
8. To develop the preventive steps that must be initiated to ensure the problems resolved once do not recur in the immediate future.

Types of Case Studies

The entire gamut of business case studies can be classified as follows:

1. Evaluative case studies—Teaching Case
2. Task- or action-oriented case studies (including project-based case studies)
3. Research-oriented case studies—Case Research

Teaching case studies are basically oriented towards developing the evaluative and analytical skills of students towards industry situations. Such case studies draw the attention of participants of the case resolution methodology on the in-depth correlative evaluation of the issues in the case study with the various related topics that the students have to study about in their classrooms. These case studies could be on issues related to human resources, industrial relations, product and process, marketing and finance management areas in business management.

Such case studies help the students mainly to examine their understanding of evaluative steps such as evaluation of the financial situation of a company or the quality aspects of its products and services, etc. The task- or action-oriented case studies dwell on business issues that call for appropriate decision-making capabilities of executives. By involving students of management studies in the resolution activity of such case studies, the skills learnt by them through the theoretical studies can be experimented in the resolution exercises.

The students can be motivated to apply their decision-making skills along with their risk management ability to make business decisions. Developing a plan of actions oriented towards the resolution of the case issues calls for effective role-play techniques as also presentation skills from the part of students; they are normally required to defend their plan of approach and decisions in front of other students and the faculty, which helps them improve their capabilities to sustain questions and criticisms, normal features in business management.

Research-based case studies, as the name suggests, involve students in research initiatives to establish a hypothesis or to disprove a common belief, which influence the progress and sustenance of business ideologies or even scientific or technical aspects of business dynamics.

These case studies normally call for prerequisites such as thorough business knowledge and enough exposure to both the theoretical and practical aspects of the issues presented in the case studies. Issues of corporate governance and social welfare functions, which have both obligatory and voluntary elements attached to them, are pursued in research studies to establish the utility purposes of such aspects, which range from free will to a compelled activity.

However, the real problem today for B-schools is the non-availability of good case studies on Indian business. Recently, it was reported that IIMs (IIM Bangalore) are resorting to appointing consultants to develop case studies on Indian enterprises, since the usage of imported case studies from foreign businesses is fast losing its relevance to the Indian business scenario, which in itself has unique features among the global economies. India, which is rated as the world's fourth-largest economy, definitely needs specific and separate approaches to the case study methodology as a pedagogical tool for B-school studies.

The Present Environment

The Academic Environment across the world is facing a major disruption on account of the global pandemic COVID-19 compounded by the unexpected war between Russia and Ukraine forcing the offline education to switch over to online/blended versions of teaching and learning process. And use of case methodology and simulation exercises are the main ingredients while maintaining the effective ways of delivering experiential learning through the use of case and case lets in an online mode of teaching ensuring student engagements and online interactive ways of knowledge dissemination. Realizing this requirement even globally reputed Institutes such as Harvard & MIT Sloan have made case method of teaching as essential parts of their online courses.

ASM Group with nearly 250 business case studies developed by its faculty over years takes pleasure in offering these cases mostly on Indian businesses through these case volumes to the faculty, students as also for Executive Education programs. The case studies are selected from ASM's Captive Case Bank as most appropriate for the current day syllabi and on Indian business scenario including select live case studies on ongoing businesses.

The case volumes also have few cases on foreign business situations basically to provide a bit of variety and correlation of issues across the globe.

The series editors and the volume authors of this volume along with ASM group of Institutes Pune India are certain that the case volumes as published will receive excellent response from the faculty and students alike in B-schools in India and abroad.

SECTION I
CASE STUDIES IN HUMAN RESOURCES

HR, Entrepreneurship, CSR, CG and Sustainability

1. Sony Pictures Network—A New PMA Philosophy
2. Determining Employee Training Needs
3. The 'Nerves of Steel'—Tackling Hard Core Issues
4. A Twist in the Tail
5. 'AI and the Ethical Dilemma'
6. 'Intense Fear Syndrome of Potential Job Loss'

1

Sony Pictures Network— A New PMA Philosophy

Introduction

Sony Pictures Networks India (SPN) is an indirect wholly-owned subsidiary of Sony Corporation, Japan. With the tagline 'Beyond Expectations' SPN has several channels including Sony Entertainment Television (SET and SET HD), one of India's leading Hindi general entertainment television channels. SPN reaches out to over 700 million viewers in India and is available in 167 countries. Sony Pictures Networks India Private Limited is in its 25th year of operations in India. Sony is a manufacturer of audio, video, communications, and information technology products for consumer and professional markets. The PESTEL/PESTLE analysis of Sony Corporation reveals a number of significant opportunities and threats that shape the electronics, gaming, entertainment, and financial services markets. Most of these external factors present opportunities that Sony can take.

Background of Sony

Japan's Sony Corporation (Sony) is the parent company. The company is mainly focused on electronics, such as audiovisual and information technology and components; games, such as PlayStation, entertainment such as motion pictures and music, and financial services such as insurance and banking. It has five segments: electronics, games, photos, and other financial services. Sony makes this one of the largest and most diverse entertainment worldwide. In the electronics segment develops, designs, manufactures, and sells various types of electronic equipment, tools, and devices for consumer and professional markets.

Indian Business Case Studies. Roopa Praveen, Dilip Aher, and Nilesh Anute, Oxford University Press. © ASM Group of Institutes, Pune, India 2022. DOI: 10.1093/oso/9780192869418.003.0001

Awards and Recognitions

The network is recognized as an employer of choice within and outside the media industry. SPN is recipient of several awards, including the 'Aon Best Employers India' Award in recognition of SPN's unique workplace culture and exceptional people practices and ranked 5th amongst India's top 50 great midsized workplace, 2017. Recipient of Adgully Digixx Award, Digital marketing excellence award, 2018, SPN consistently ranking amongst India's Top 10 Companies with Best Health & Wellness Practices by SHRM & CGP Partners, listed by Working Mother & AVTAR Award in 2019 as one of the 100 Best Companies for Women in India and adjudged one of India's great workplaces by the great place to work institute.

Sony's HRM Policy

Sony HRM policy is to manage their employees and to be successful. Because it considers the variation in different regions. Sony, encourages their employees to participate in decision-making, so that the company 'public meeting' in each unit provides opportunities for employees to give their opinion.

Sony provides education and skills training for workers in different countries and business sectors. But there are different training systems in different regions. Kio Morita, founder of Sony Corporation, once mentioned the secret of success is just the way they treat their employees. When he was president of Sony, said new employees and all employees who are lucky enough to find jobs and to decide personally if he has spent his lifetime working with Sony.

The Purpose of Human Resource Management Policy in Sony

Sony values innovative approach, communication between management and workers are essential if the management transfer policy for employees and employers to encourage their opinions. Sony puts a high priority on communication between management and individual employees. Since fiscal 2005, Sony CEO Howard Stringer, was visiting the Sony world to communicate directly with employees at public meetings and other opportunities for dialogue to create. Sony aims to create a workplace that respects human rights and equal employment opportunities for people with best of their abilities.

Re-engineering the Employee Evaluation Process

For effective performance management system, everyone has invested in its success. From the newest employee to the highest-ranking executive, everyone involved should be aware of the system, how it operates, and why it adds true value to your organization. Though the HR department will be primarily responsible for designing and implementing the performance management system and rolling it out across the organization, managers need to play their part to ensure its success.

Recently a SPN group company has evolved so rapidly that they are feeling the need to change the way they hire, assess, and appraise talent. Just over a month ago, in November 2019, Sony Pictures Network India joined a growing band of companies that are re-engineering their performance management systems, doing away with the bell curve and regency bias and forms and static procedures. SPN, which is in its 25th year of operations in India and has 24 channels and 1,200-plus employees, has evolved a new philosophy and practice on talent-related initiatives.

Need to change the performance management system? Several companies are now doing away with the bell curve and going in for continuous feedback. But implementation is often difficult as managers have to be trained.

The traditional system was structured as a top-down, linear, bi-annual appraisal process with talent discussions happening twice annually. But in order to maintain leadership in the industry, the company became innovative, agile, and updated. While embracing agility, it focused for re-examine values and the way we evaluate performance.

As a precursor to the implementation of new growth agenda, SPN launched the six new values of SPN and crafted a simple, relatable e-version of values which every member of SPN can imbibe in their day-to-day life. And, to stay aligned to these values, we re-engineered our performance philosophy.

Check-in for Change—a brand tag for a new agile performance management framework called **Connect-Plan-Mentor** (CPM). The essence of the CPM Framework is:

Connect to Reflect. This is about setting clear goals and milestones and checking on it.

Plan for Future. This is about agile recognition of performance development needs.

Mentor for Development—regular conversations between employee and manager on performance and values as well as data and science-based talent decisions.

CPM framework initiates check-ins with managers six times in a year, which leads to multi-point data on performance and provides a holistic view of performance. This, in turn, leads to insight-based decisions for employers and helps to map productivity. Detailed individual charts enable managers to assess/monitor gaps in performance on a real-time basis and provide timely feedback and support. These give each leader a perspective on employee potential and performance round the year and help them take apt reward decisions.

SPN created sufficient awareness and understanding about the new system within the top management before an official launch. Functional heads were educated to get them on board before an overall launch.

SPN also invested in technology-enabled change—through individual passports and QR codes leading to videos by CEO and CHRO along with live broadcast by leadership team. There were deep immersion sessions across the organization as well as a personalized approach—100% leaders and employees were taken through the journey of change management schedule.

Given the amalgamation of industries and the fluidity of talent in these cases, companies are always on the lookout for talent from across genres, and the talent pool management teams actively recruit people outside the media & entertainment industry.

In addition, the talent mix already comprises nearly 70% millennial, a nod to the rapidly changing demographics of the workforce today. Given that SPN is also in the era of the gig economy, it leverages on its talent workforce for many projects. As part of its talent development program schedules, they are also upskilling their current employees by providing alternate learning experiences, reverse mentoring, expert talks, and design thinking workshops, among other initiatives.

Sony plans and strategies reflect different depending on their unique vision and mission. Strategies, plans, and even their threats failures contribute to the company. Sony Corporation to take into account not only new technologies, new products and automation, but the environment is healthy. Human resource management is even possible cultural and national differences. Policies should distinguish IHRM organization and integration of all units. Sony is creating an example to explain. Human Resources supports the general conclusion that human resource management for the benefit of employees and human resources activities in accordance with the strategic goals of Sony. Sony managers held on the need for staff and delegates tasks to assess these good impressions on the leaders and they believe the company delegated authority, which in turn increases job security for frames. Programs for different levels of employees is to create a team spirit among employees and a culture in which everyone is entitled to make progress in the promotion.

Conclusions

One of the expressions we hear most often is 'employee-centric'. In fairness, this can have more than one meaning, but the intention remains the same for each: to create an environment that encourages and supports people to bring their best selves to work. **Employee-centric thinking** describes operating in a way that puts the employee experience front and centre. Performance management is an ever-evolving field. The more we learn, the better we can adapt our performance management systems to make our companies healthier, more motivational places to work. Companies who fall behind lose out to their competitors. They also run the risk of losing their best performers along the way.

Case Questions

1. How performance and engagement worked together to achieve the strategic goal in SPN?

2. How do you link frequent *performance management* process learning and feedback to promotion strategy and decisions?

3. Do you think continuous performance management in SPN is well acknowledged by the employee's then traditional process?

References

http://panmore.com/sony-corporation-pestel-pestle-analysis-recommendations.
https://www.tlnt.com/what-you-need-to-make-your-performance-management-program-work/
https://www.ukessays.com/essays/business/strategic-human-resources-managem
ent-of-sony-business-essay.php

2

Determining Employee Training Needs

A Case Study on Leig India Ltd.

Learning Objectives

Understanding the purpose of training need analysis. Learning the steps in conducting training need analysis. Appreciating the use of competency models for training needs assessments. Developing a process of TNA

Synopsis

Leig India Group is a multi-unit, multi-interest group with above Rs 500 crore turnover. Over the last seven decades, Leig had emerged as a well-diversified group with manufacturing facilities in South India, the group had diversified operations ranging from spinning, engineering to building materials. It was one of the few companies, which had not only survived for more than seven decades but also done well changing with the changing industrial environment. It had stood the test of time with a good and steady growth rate. Leig Spinning Mills Limited (LSML) was the flagship company of Leig India contributing over 90% of its turnover.

Leig India is a traditional Coimbatore-based organization and does not have a well-developed HR function. The average age of the employees at the executive level was 45 years. Most of them had been with the organization for over 10 years. The number of people retiring was increasing every year. The company was losing 2–5% of the employees due to retirement and many of them were still continuing after retirement without holding any position. Hiring was increased and the new entrants needed

Indian Business Case Studies. Roopa Praveen, Dilip Aher, and Nilesh Anute, Oxford University Press. © ASM Group of Institutes, Pune, India 2022. DOI: 10.1093/oso/9780192869418.003.0002

to be given training, something more than the usual induction. With no training budget and a formal system for training and development, the newly recruited HR Manager develops the training need assessment process.

Case Details

Leig was started when the textile industry was booming in Coimbatore. LSML had a well-established system and ran like well-oiled machinery. Senior executives and top-level executives were primarily the decision makers who were given full autonomy. Though it was a public listed company, the major shareholders were the family members of the founder. The business was run like a family business with family members controlling its operations; both chairman and managing director were from the family.

The group first started as a textile mill—LSML in 1962 and subsequently diversified into engineering and building products. The promoters hold 40.02% of the shares. LSML contributed over 430 crores to the 500-crore turnover company with domestic sales of Rs 331.47 crores and exports of Rs 98.77 crores. The corporate office was located in Coimbatore and the three units were in Andhra Pradesh. One was in Dindigul district of Tamil Nadu. The production capacity of the mills was 12 tons per day.

LSML manufactured 100% combed cotton Yarn and Leig Electric and Industries Limited manufactured equipment for textile and motor industry. Also, yarn-conditioning systems, centralized vacuum cleaning systems, metal and spark diversion systems, waste collection systems, premium/high-efficiency electric motors, alternators, and DG Sets. It also supplied AC/DC motors and traction changing pointing machines to Indian Railways. Leig India Arteriors Limited manufactured UPVC doors, UPVC windows, UPVC casement doors, sliding doors, and ventilators targeted at medium and premium segment consumers.

Competition was getting tougher and the company had to adapt to the changes if it had to exist. The average age of its executives was around 45 years. Most of them were there for almost 15–20 years. Most of them were retiring with 2–5% leaving every year. The company was interested in increasing its productivity and product quality. The chief executives realized that if the company continued to operate in the traditional way it would not be able to adapt to the changes. Leig was hiring in a big way. The chief executives decided to have more professionals take charge. One of the departments that need urgent attention was the HR department. The HR manager was to retire within a year. The chief executives decided to hire a young professional to manage the HR activities. They hired Mr R Ashok, a 35-year-old person as the HR manager. He was to establish an HR department that was more than just an administrative department.

Human Resources Department

HR department was more of an administrative department focusing on compensation, canteen facilities, hiring, and ensuring legal compliance. HR department as it existed was only three employees. At the corporate office at present there was only one HR manager under VP-HR and an HR executive. The HR department handled:

- Recruitment and selection of employees after assessing the need for manpower
- Training and development programmes including identifying the needs and arranging for training
- Administration of compensation and benefits
- Conduct of performance appraisals
- Gratuity and superannuation fund
- Revision of wage of all group companies

Development/frames and modifies company policies like the HR policy, Safety Policy, and Employee Code of Conduct and ensures implementation of the same.

HR Objectives (3M/3R)

- Maximize employee capabilities.
- Maximize employee performance at work.

- Maximize production and productivity through employee engagement activities.
- Reduce attrition rate
  o Reduce absenteeism rate
  o Reduce accidents

A comprehensive HR manual of Leig laid down the procedures, systems, rules, and policies of the functioning of the HR department.

Training and Development at Leig

Of the total number of 246 office employees working in Leig, 40 were at the corporate office, 11 in the R&D division in Pollachi, rest of them at the four units of LSML and around 5000 workers, both contract and permanent workers were employed at the four units. The training programme at Leig was developed on the basis of the following objectives:

- build a skilled, well-trained, and professional workforce
- develop and strengthen organizational leadership
- adopt current best management practices
- encourage innovation and continuous improvements in performance
- enable new employees to share a common understanding of their role
- impart required knowledge to managers at all levels to effectively exercise their delegated authorities and responsibilities
- ensure that the employees at all levels acquire and update and improve the knowledge, skills, and competencies related to their position/role and area
- apply best and competitive practices of the industry
- enable managers to align learning with the achievement of the organizational objectives

Training Policy at Leig India Limited

Training and development programmes were based on the needs identified. Employees attended external development programmes organized or conducted by educational institutions, professional associations like Southern India Mills Association (SIMA), South India Textile and Research Association (SITRA), Coimbatore Management Association (CMA), Confederation of Indian Industry (CII), etc. Training needs were identified on the basis of the appraisal forms. Internal training was mostly organized prior to audit or accreditation. Majority of the other training and developmental programmes organized were technical for the workers or general in nature like on health awareness, meditation, well-being, etc. The rule for conducting training programmes for staff and workmen were as follows:

Staff—Every staff was to be given two days training either internally or externally; Workmen—Every workman was to be given one day training on the topics of skill development, knowledge improvement, and attitude. SIMA or SITRA gave most of the technical training. Trainers were also invited. Most of the training and development programmes attended by employees were by external organizations, educational institutes, and industry associations like CMA, CII, etc. in and around the city.

Identification of Training Needs

Training needs were identified based on the performance appraisals. The second part of the appraisal form contained details of the development plans of the employee. Based on the training needs, training calendar and budget were prepared by the unit HR and approved at corporate office. Training and development were becoming increasingly important to organizations for achieving competitive advantage. At Leig technical training by SIMA and SITRA were organized for workers and those involved in the production process.

Ashok working on creating a process of training need identification realized that there was no proper budget allocated separately for training. A need was felt to have a system of training assessment so that the training and development programmes of the company are planned and budgeted. A systematic and planned training programme means judicial investment in employees and providing them a learning environment so that they update their knowledge, learn, and improve their skills which they will be transferring to their job resulting in high performance for both the individual and the organization. Ashok developed a training need assessment tool, which was reviewed and awaited the approval from the VP-HR and chief executives.

Training Needs Analysis (TNA) at Leig Spinning Mills

Ashok examined in detail the job descriptions of the employees and had a series of interview with the top management, heads of departments, and the employees. As the first phase he developed an extensive procedure for identifying training needs for Leig Spinning Mills. Ashok developed a process to be used for new hires and existing employees till grade 8. The tool could be used at the time of selection.

The following factors indicated training or development needs of LSML employees:

A. Development of employee/management skills to fill a current need
  - New hires
  - Reassignments
  - Promotions
  - Employee relations/organizational problems
  - Performance problems
  - Production problems
  - Safety problems
B. Quality deficiencies
C. Meet changing needs
  - New technology
  - New equipment or programmes
  - Modernization of equipment
  - Laws and regulations
D. Career development for meeting future need
  - Employees' requests
  - Career enhancement plans

He identified tools and techniques for determining specific training needs. The sources of information collected were from—job description—the narrative statement of the major activities involved in performing the job and the conditions under which these activities were performed were analysed.

Questionnaires/interviews for task analysis—determining KSA required to perform the tasks and difficulty analysis and evaluation of the task based on importance. Appraisal reviews and performance standards—Objectives of the tasks of the job and the standards by which they would be judged were used to identify performance discrepancies.

Process of TNA at LSML

Ashok proposed allocating a budget for training and development. The process followed for TNA was given as under:

- The job description was collected that is the narrative statement of the major activities involved in performing the job and the conditions under which these activities are performed
- Task analysis that is the tasks that are to be performed was collected
- Task evaluation was done in terms of degree of importance
- Knowledge, Skills and Attitude (KSA) to perform each job were identified
- The list of competencies to perform the job successfully was prepared department wise for each position
- Gap analysis was carried out, that is, difference between the required and available level of competency
- Based on this the training to be given was determined
- This tool was also to be used for selection and appraisal

1. Finalising job description and task analysis—(interview the employees of each department)
   - Interview questions:
     i. Does the JD given include all your responsibilities and duties and tasks?
     ii. If no, what else would you include and what would you exclude?
     iii. What tasks are performed?
     iv. How frequently are they performed?

2. Task evaluation
   - Interview question
     i. How important is each task/how important is the task?
        a. Not very important—Poor performance on this task will not affect the overall performance of the job.
        b. Somewhat important—Poor performance on this task will have a moderate effect on overall performance of the job.
        c. Important—Poor performance on this task will have an effect on the overall performance of the job.
        d. Very important—Poor performance on this task will have a serious effect on the overall performance of the job.
     ii. Importance at the time of hire
        a. Not important—A person requires no specific capability in this area when hired. Training will be provided for an individual to become proficient in the area.
        b. Somewhat important—A person must have only a basic capability in this area when hired. Experience on the job or training is the primary method for becoming proficient in this area.
        c. Important—A person must be completely proficient in this area when hired. There is time or training available only to provide 'fine tuning' once the person is on the job.
        d. Very important—A person must be completely proficient in this area when hired. There is no time or training procedure available to help an individual become proficient in this area after being placed on the job.
3. Determining KSAs
   a. What knowledge is needed to perform the task?
   b. What skills are necessary to perform the task?
   c. Develop a list of competencies for each department level wise.
4. Determining Training Needs
   a. What aspects of your job do you find satisfying?
   b. What would you change about your job if you could?
   c. Which aspects of your work interest you least?
   d. How difficult is each task?
   e. Which aspects of your work do you find most difficult?

    f. Have you sometimes found it difficult to do your job because of a lack of technical knowledge?

    g. What kinds of training are available?

    h. What training have you had?

    i. What training do you think would be useful in your present position?

    j. What training do you wish you had received in the past?

    k. Have you any skills or knowledge that is not being used in your job?

    l. How do you know if you are doing a good job?

    m. What do you think other people think about your performance?

    n. When do you feel most pressured?

5. Analysing the data and giving suggestions for types of training.

Develop a tool to be used during selection (new hires) and appraisal (existing employees) or to identify specific training needs.

Training Need Assessment Tools

The following tools were developed for training need assessment at Leig Spinning Mills Ltd. There are five forms.

- Form 1 assessed the gap in the competencies or KSAs of each employee by the score arrived by taking the difference between the desired level of the competency and the available level. The employee and 2 superiors filled the form as is with the appraisals. If the gap can be bridged through training, then appropriate steps were to be taken.
- The employee filled form 2 and it concerns the task he/she performs when in his/her position. This form is thus an analysis of the task and requires employees to rank each task on the basis of priority, the level of difficulty, and frequency performed. The tool enables to identify specific training needs.
- Form 3 was filled and maintained by the HR department. It is a record of department wise training needs of the employees. This will help the HR department in organizing the training and development programmes.

- Form 4 was also a record to be maintained by the HR department. It gives a detailed account of the training programmes organized in a given year along with the cost incurred. It also details the feedback on the trainers and trainees.
- Form 5 was a record of the training each employee has undergone in a year. It also has details of the employee feedback of the programme and trainer; and the trainer feedback of the employee/trainee. The tools are enclosed in Annexure C of the case.

Case Questions

1. How was the training need analysis done at LSML?

2. Describe in detail the five forms and whether it is sufficient for assessing the training needs?

3. Should LSML follow competency-model based training assessment?

4. Compare the TNA suggested by Mr Ashok with the earlier TNA that LSML followed?

5. Can you develop a process for assessing the training needs for LSML?

6. How would you conduct a needs assessment for the Leig India group?

Bibliography

Blanchard, P. Nick, Thacker, James, V. and Ram, V. Anand. (2012). Effective Training, 4/e; New Delhi: Pearson Education.

Noe, A. Raymond and Kodwani, D. Amitabh. (2012). Employee Training and Development, 5/e; New Delhi: Tata McGraw-Hill.

Janakiram, B. (2007). Training and Development; New Delhi: Biztantra.

3

The 'Nerves of Steel'—Tackling Hard Core Issues

Case study on Entrepreneurial Challenges

Learning Objectives

1. The real issues and opportunities in the successful management of any enterprise especially when there are issues related to intra per-sonal relations countering professional approach are very well dealt in this case study.
2. Emotional intelligence is put to acid test in you feel that whatever you do or wish to do may not help you out. This case study gets in to real ground level issues in emotional intelligence capabilities.

Synopsis

If the readers are entrepreneurs by career choice this case study will help in dealing with real shop level issues which are not usually taught in B schools. The case study red hot brings to limelight real issues bothering the entrepreneur and the enterprise.

Case Details

Mr Mahir Latkar was a self-made entrepreneur with lot of zeal and ambi-tion, with commitment to excel in his maiden enterprise 'The Red Hot'.

Coming from a rural background he was a little conservative and scep-tical about people around him and needed to ensure that his basic policies

Indian Business Case Studies. Roopa Praveen, Dilip Aher, and Nilesh Anute, Oxford University Press. © ASM Group of Institutes, Pune, India 2022. DOI: 10.1093/oso/9780192869418.003.0003

and principles were followed by one and all. He was naturally concerned with interpersonal contacts and relations.

Mr Ramesh Pable was a childhood friend in whom Mahir had lots of faith and trust and looked at him for radical advice from time to time.

But it was Ravi. for months, Mahir had been grappling with the relationship. Ravi was from Vita, a small village in Nasik, where he produced flyers and leaflets for various political parties, a temple, some shops that were launching a new this or that. Ravi's visualizing and designing skills were respected and this fetched him a few rupees. But Mahir wanted him to complete his graduation, 'and after that I will get you a job', he had assured.

With a lot of difficulty, Ravi had scraped through some sort of distant learning package and Mahir hired him at Red Dot, which was in the business of website development and interactive marketing. Red Dot was Mahir's brainchild, which he had set up in 2001.

Ravi did not have any formal training in designing, but his work was brilliant. For three years, Mahir put him through all kinds of design work and groomed him to a level where he had overcome his language barrier and had started taking client briefs himself. But, during the past one year, something about this relationship had changed.

Uddhav, strategic advisor to Red Dot and Mahir, had not missed the anxiety building up in Mahir. Yesterday, he had asked him: 'Name one thing about Ravi that is bothersome.' And Mahir had said, 'He has come to "know" me and my style, and also knows I will never ask him to go.' Uddhav had smiled and said, 'Then it is simple, no? Just ask him to go.' Mahir had reacted to that with a convulsed shake of his shoulders, 'What do you mean? How can I ask him to go? He has an old mother, that rascal! I think more of her than him!' Uddhav said, 'The mother is fine, Mahir. send her maintenance money, that's OK.'

But answer this: 'when a person has been working for more than 4–5 years with you, it's time to ask why he is still with you. Do you have a real answer?' And Uddhav had left him to deal with it.

Now back in his office, Mahir realized it was complacency that had killed Ravi's creativity; he was delivering all right, but his delivery was bad; clients (in Mumbai, Nagpur, Baroda) were unhappy. Ravi cribbed saying he could not manage people. Things had come to a head last week when Mahir had admonished him. A job was due at 4:00 p.m., and at 3:30 p.m.

Ravi was relaxing on his chair listening to film Music. 'I have not given the job any thought,' he told Mahir nonchalantly. 'Sorry, I cannot think.'

That was when Mahir decided to discuss the matter with Uddhav. Ravi had never talked like this ever. 'Ravi, is a star. He knows it,' he told Uddhav. 'He is a part of the reason why Red Dot is successful. It's not as if success has gone to his head. It has just dulled him. He is not only producing mediocre work, he is also delaying the whole system. Worse, he does not care!'

Today, Uddhav and Mahir were going to have a chat with Ravi. Since Uddhav was the mentor and advisor at Red Dot, they had spent enough time, whole of last week, talking about what needed to be done.

When Ravi came in, Uddhav began gently, 'Ravi, you need to take time off. Don't come to work for 15 days. Chill a bit, meet friends, adjust your world view to reality outside your work life. Put your feet up and think about life, the universe and the dog. Read a bit, catch a movie; do what always wanted to do.

You know what, your work is deteriorating and this is a surprise for Mahir and me. Perhaps you feel jaded doing the same thing over and over again. Maybe you have even outgrown Red Dot.

May be you just need a fresh challenge? All this you need to figure out, for only you can. Maybe you simply need a new mountain to climb and feel good life ... We don't know, Ravi. That is why we are asking you to go and find out why you are jaded.'

Ravi sat there, one leg out, both arms clutching the outward knee, rocking himself back and forth. Snatches of sentences and words were flying at him, 'You have potential ... Red Dot values you ... Your colleagues think highly of you.' Now Mahir was saying, 'And if you decide that you don't want to come back at all, that would be OK too.'

'Why?' asked Ravi gruffly. Uddhav said, 'We spent a lot of time debating exactly that question. Neither Mahir nor I want you to go. Then it struck us that you have actually become a habit here, just as Red Dot has become a habit in your life; you are simply going through the motions and not brining anything to the table.

This, we realized, was why you were not contributing. Not creating. Not sizzling. Worse, you have stopped giving, not just to Red Dot, but to friends who you grew up with here—Pakya, Vinoo, Kailas. We have seen a huge mountain of doubt and apprehension in you, which blocks everything. This is also hindering the growth of Red Dot and your friends here. So, take 10 days off, climb this mountain of self-doubt; overcome it, kill it, summit it to see what's happened ... and come back and tell us, do you want to claim our mountain or yours.'

Not Ravi, but the whole of Red Dot's challenge was unusual, yet interesting. Ten years of liberalization had blessed the big metros with abundance; smartly clad MNC managers zipped around talking about 'moving India' to the small towns, taking the benefits of the largess to the 'lesser Indians'.

Even before India had woken up to moving to tier II and III cities, Mahir had done it, by recruiting from small towns like Sangli, Kolhapur, Ahmednagar, Beed, Jalgaon, etc. and from developing colleges in Ahmednagar, Nagpur, etc. where the youngsters were passionate about a profession. He trained them from scratch in creative design, HTML, technical knowledge for Web-based applications, quality assurance, etc.

People had called him mad for the seeming risk he was taking as he was neck-deep in loans. But what it reaped for Red Dot was stability, loyalty, commitment, and, most of all, a commonality of ethos and ethics, which was precious to Mahir. From the client's perspective, it assured a more dependable and consistent delivery team. In an era, when people switched jobs, cities, countries, partners, employers, Mahir continued to have employees who stuck on for at least 3–4 years.

He achieved this using an emotional connect, through their native language—Red Dot buzzed with four different dialects of Marathi, Milind Ingle (piped), Sandeep Jhare/Salil Kulkarni poetry and the breathtaking fragrance of pitla bhaat and foad lela kaanda that the bachelor boys enjoyed.

In turn, for all these men and women from the smallest towns of Maharashtra, Red Dot was a safe haven, where they got challenging assignments, where their skills grew, they were appreciated and, finally, they could send a decent packet home every month. They didn't need to go to the US.

Of course, a couple of Jalgaon boys picked up skills at Red Dot and left for other jobs in the US. But Mahir did not grudge them that, and he also knew that others were dreaming of doing likewise. But he needed to ensure that the time and effort he invested in his team did not go into building the future of some other company. So, he needed to give them the right opportunities, so that not only did their technical skills grow, but also their emotional, managerial, and personal skills.

One way to enable their growth was to let Red Dot staffers interface with clients. This was becoming more critical in recent times, especially after a few clients commented that Red Dot had only one person they could rely on Mahir. It then became imperative that he build a client-facing team to reassure his more mature clients that Red Dot's team could attend to their needs. However, like many self-driven entrepreneurs, Mahir sought personal satisfaction alongside professional.

And this was where Uddhav was immensely valuable for Mahir. Uddhav knew why Mahir close the kind of people he did. Uddhav knew the effort and investment Mahir made in these people. Uddhav knew what Mahir's orientation to work was. And Mahir knew Red Dot.

Red Dot had been built literally from scratch, and, today, it continued to reflect that personality. However, it was a personality, work method, and way of doing business that could not be scaled. Red Dot needed to grow and it needed several people who could manage its business, clients, ideating, business mining, and image management.

But the truth was that Red Dot would soon need to grow in areas that Mahir would not be able to supervise personally or be a part of there just wasn't that much time for him to do everything. For example, the circles he had been drawing around Ravi to groom him, skill him, grow him, monitor him was something Ravi took for granted as something that was natural from a fellow native towner. But for Mahir, all this was far more than time; it was energy which he was not willing to dissipate.

He wanted to 'add value' to every step, he wanted to 'Personally re-spond' to clients, he wanted to be the personal friend, guide, and phi-losopher to every of his 54 brethren and sisters from Maharashtra. This was creating small bottlenecks, which while not disrupting, caused grief. Mahir kept asking Uddhav, 'Can you groom one or two people to take over what I am doing, in a manner that I understand and appreciate? In a manner that I believe it ought to be done? In a manner that I find my values being upheld?'

Yet, Mahir changed his mind: 'Hey! I am not sure I want this done, man. That interaction with "Ojas-The-Errant" and Heads Up has shown me the error of delegating top management.' But the very next minute he shook his head vigorously denying that thought, and said, 'No, you go ahead and tell me what to do.' Uddhav had designed yet another class-room workshop to take the 10 staffers on the workshop, forward, which was scheduled for the next day.

This was the day and Pable too arrived at 10:00 a.m. to meet Mahir and demanded his slow roasted coffee. 'Just follow me … you will get coffee and a free lesson, come,' said Mahir and took him into the audiovisual room where Uddhav's classroom was beginning.

Gesturing to a confused Pable to be quiet and watch, Mahir text messaged his assistant, 'OK, now the special coffee please.'

Uddhav (in session): Say, we have a colleague who we hired because he is brilliant. Then one day he becomes dull, short changes the client, behaves badly, does not deliver 100%, client is annoyed. What should Red Dot do?

The client does not realize that the 'search' feature is keeping the serve engaged and could be at a cost to another visitor who is in a hurry but finds the pages are slow to load. You, as Red Dot, know why the page is slow to upload. Now, from the client's point of view (whose website it is), both visitors to the site are being served.

Put issues on the table

Only Red Dot knows that the process can be streamlined (and should be streamlined) for better business results. Will you present this as a problem to be solved, to the client?

Kalpana: Is this a billable job? (Much argument follows over the correctness of this).

Uddhav: You are the service provider and you are committed to provide least cost, best option to every customer; that is what your motto says, now tell me.

Kailaas: I disagree. I have been doing 'search' stuff for the last seven years and there is no money in this. And it is not our focus too. If I fix everything that you are saying, then our clients may pay Rs. 5,000 for that. The next client doesn't want to pay and uses Google's free tool instead. Then?

Uddhav: Then? Then, the client finds out that you knew the way out but didn't tell him. Should the client sack us or give us a warning? See, you feel the money isn't worth slaving over this client. But when you took on the client, you swore to deliver 100% on all counts. So, where did this individual assessment of cost benefit come from? 'Serve the client' includes everything, no? Including behaving well?

Pakya: See, there are other aspects of 'search' that can be rewarding for a client and cannot be done by using Google and are based on analytics and tweaking content based on intelligence. This is something that can result in value add, if explained property to a client.

Uddhav: Aa-ha! Now why is this pleasing? Hmm. See how we have moved from understanding a problem to understanding client to client comfort ... so what will you tell the client so that he does not imagine that you are shortchanging him?

Hanif: He must study the user behaviours carefully to see their segmentation as well as their usage, and how he can serve this better.

Uddhav: You have three minutes, form two teams. I am your client, a Fortune 500 company. Please present to me why you will do what you will do.

As the teams presented and fumbled, Uddhav tweaked and structured their script bit by bit. 'If you say that, won't your client think you are unsure? He is your client, he is coming to you for solutions, you have to be confident about what you are selling! Meghna, you are the client, you have two minutes only ... why is Kailaas's approach not convincing you?'

Uddhav was deftly moving from problem definition to problem presentation, to how to present PROBLEM A from the point of view of the client rather than the Red Dot point of view so that the client understands exactly what the manager was saying.

How to listen to the client before speaking; how to use the keywords and concepts that the client is talking about to win conversation and grab attention ('It's about listening to the client, hearing his words, hearing the tone of his words!') how to identify the key concerns of a client and to attend to those first, before moving on to what Red Dot has in mind; how to make the client win rather than make Red Dot win in a conversation, so that business for Red Dot increases.

'Remember, the client is not right because he is king; he is right because he owns the problem. And as long as he has a problem, you need to be there; till you set it right ... working to get the fee cheque is not why we are here.'

Mahir: And yes, about that employee who misbehaved; I won't sack him. Never. I will correct him till he buys into the correction. Once he is a good egg, he is free to go. Anybody who has worked here even two years carries a bit of Red Dot in him. He is a Red Dot product! When he goes away he continues to carry Red Dot with him. He had better carry it well, I say!

At 12 noon, the class ended, Mahir introduced Uddhav to Pable, 'Meet Uddhav, our strategic advisor. He refines and redefines our ideas by making them simpler.' Pable shook hands most vigorously in expression of his joy. Then he said to Mahir, 'I now see that you can keep your employees in sync with your principles if that is what you believe! Congratulations! I just woke up to the coffee!'

Case Questions

1. What are entrepreneurial qualities which Mahir needs to improve and execute?

2. What strategy do you recommend for Red Hot for its sustainability and growth? Explain the strategic options available to Mr Mahir.

3. What according to you is important 'Employee Performance' or 'Loyalty'? How do you restructure the HR policies of Red Hot to achieve a 'Performance Driven Loyalty?'

4

A Twist in the Tail

A Case Study on Corporate Governance—Tata vs Mistry

Learning Objectives

Managing business ideologies and long-term vision and missions in very large business conglomerates have been a real challenge with changing times and global market expansions.

Time and again conflicts arise at board levels since the next generation CEOs while respecting the overall group ethos and visions find it essential to bend a bit backwards on occasions where it is difficult to adhere strictly to laid out norms. Even though the intention behind is not to harm the group's value systems followed over several decades but such CEO level decisions are frowned upon by the old timers who are always sceptical of visionary drifts which according to their wisdom cannot be tolerated.

Some such issues have been the basis for board room disagreements at times leading to full-blown wars leading to unceremonious removal of CEOs who violate the historical norms even if it is in the interests of the business.

It is therefore interesting for the students and practising executives to learn from this case study the generic issues involved in such board room battles leading to utter confusion of appropriate way of managing large businesses effectively over generation gaps.

Synopsis

Tata empire is a huge conglomerate from salt to software manufacturing, with massive underlying structure.

Indian Business Case Studies. Roopa Praveen, Dilip Aher, and Nilesh Anute, Oxford University Press. © ASM Group of Institutes, Pune, India 2022. DOI: 10.1093/oso/9780192869418.003.0004

Tata Sons is the holding company of the group with two-thirds of shares held by various Tata family trusts. Mr Mistry's father Mr Shapoorji Pallonji is the second-largest stakeholder in the Tata Group with 18.5% share in Tata Sons making them the largest individual shareholder in the holding company of the Tata empire.

From 1990 to 2009, Mistry served as the director of Tata Elxsi Limited and Tata Power until 2006. On 1 September 2006, he joined the board of Tata Sons, after his father's retirement from Tata Group. He was named the director of several Tata companies in addition to his duties with Pallonji Group. In 2010, Mistry was tasked to find the successor for the position of chairman held by Ratan Tata as he decided to retire a year later.

Ironically, the choice was a big surprise as Cyrus Mistry, being part of the selection committee, was appointed as the successor to Ratan Tata. It was announced as an anonymous and favourite choice by Ratan Tata (*Hindustan Times*, 2016). It was announced that Mistry would take over as the chairman a year later, thus completing the entire transition process.

In Cyrus Mistry's case, Tata's sacked Mistry from the position of group chairman on 24 October 2016 after a stint of 45 months, without any explanation at that moment. It was a big surprise and a shock wave to the corporate world. The picture at Bombay House, Tata Headquarters, was unique with sudden burst of this news, where this decision was taken. The resolution to sack Mistry was decided in minutes at the cold meeting held at Bombay House. Stock markets tumbled the next day with this sudden ouster news (*The Economic Times*, 2016, 25 October).

Later Mistry was sacked as chairman of all Tata Group of Companies. All his close associates were also sidelined and forced to step down from their ranks across the Tata Group. It led to a full-scale collision between Ratan Tata Group and Mistry faction. It was a deep mystery to Mistry on why suddenly the tables turned against him on a fine day (*Livemint*, 2016, 25 October).

Everything was kept internally until the news exploded on 24 October 2016 Tata's explained that the growing trust deficit, repeated departures from culture and the ethos of group were the reasons behind Mistry's removal.

The board also named Ratan Tata as the interim chairman of the group. A new panel was set up to find the next chairman in four months. Later, in January 2017, Tata's appointed N. Chandrasekaran as the group chairman. He was with Tata Consultancy Services (TCS) for three decades. He was appointed to the Tata board in October 2016 only. Mistry replied to the Tata board on his sacking by saying, 'shocked beyond words' and 'unparalleled in the annals of corporate history' (*India Today*, 2016, 27 October). He further added: The sudden action and lack of explanation has led to all manner of speculation and has done my and the group's reputation immeasurable harm. The letter is to emphasize the total lack of corporate governance and a failure of the directors to discharge their fiduciary duty to stakeholders of Tata Sons and the group companies. It was later acknowledged publicly by Ratan Tata that the key reason for the fallout and the big decision was Mistry's style of functioning, poor governance, and conflict of interest.

Case Details

The friction started way back in 2014 with Mistry's solo decision-making style, ignoring the Tata Sons board. Several of Mistry's business decisions, such as the sale of Indian hotels in overseas and the move to shut down the UK steel operations, did not go well with Ratan Tata. The move to shut down the UK steel business was highly criticized in Britain and was seen as a setback to Ratan Tata. These were considered as Ratan Tata's legacy which he undertook during his stint as group chairman. Tata's wanted to turn around the loss-making business than selling it, but Mistry had different plans altogether.

During Mistry's tenure as an executive chairman, dividend income (apart from TCS) declined continuously, but staff costs doubled. All this would have resulted in losses but survived due to TCS dividend; thus there was an increasing dependence of Tata Sons on TCS. Mistry did not show concern on these issues, which the board did not like. There was a conflict of interest issue with Mistry associated with his former family company Shapoorji Pallonji even after the appointment as the chairman of the Tata Group. Contracts worth 20 billion were handed to Pallonji Constructions in TCS and Tata Motors. Mistry was also seen as an underperformer. He was a slow learner and not equipped to take quick decisions. Mistry had spent the first three years understanding the Tata empire and its underlying functions as chairman. He has been building knowledge base about specific domains to ask the right questions and understanding geopolitics, technology, and societal issues at the Tata empire. Clearly, there was a fundamental disconnect between Mistry and Ratan Tata in leadership and working style.

The biggest allegation against Mistry was that he misled the chairman selection committee in 2011, by making false statements about his plans for the Tata Group and an elaborate management structure for managing the Tata Group empire. Even after four years of helm, Mistry did not fulfil any of his plans nor the management structure for which he was ultimately selected as the chairman.

The break up was when Mistry decided to acquire Welspun Renewables Energy company at 95 billion for which questions remained over the extent to which the boards of Tata Power and Tata Sons were kept in the loop and supportive.

The break-up was not a smooth one; it created a bad blood between both the parties and finally reached the tribunal. The final showdown between two factions has reached till the law corridors of National Company Law Tribunal (NCLT). On 20 December 2016, Mistry moved NCLT alleging oppression and mismanagement by Tata's on his sudden expulsion and also the interference of Ratan Tata and N. A. Soonawala in the governance of Tata Sons. A day earlier, on 19 December 2016 Mistry disassociated from the Tata empire by resigning from all boards of the Tata group.

The Steps Taken

20 December 2016: Two Mistry family backed investment firms, Cyrus Investments Pvt Ltd and Sterling Investments Corporation Pvt Ltd, move the NCLT Mumbai, alleging oppression of minority shareholders and mismanagement by Tata Sons. They also challenged Mistry's removal.

6 March 2017: NCLT Mumbai sets aside the plea of the two investment firms of Mistry family over maintainability issue, citing they didn't meet the criteria 10% ownership in a company for the filing of a case of alleged oppression of minority shareholders under the Companies Act.

The Mistry family owns 18.4% stake in the closely-held Tata Sons but the holding is less than 3% if preferential shares are excluded.

17 April 2017: NCLT Mumbai also rejects plea by the two investment firm's plea seeking waiver in the criteria of having at least 10%

ownership in a company for filing case of alleged oppression of minority shareholders.

The **NCLT** has primary jurisdiction whereas **NCLAT** has appellate jurisdiction. **NCLAT** is a higher forum than **NCLT**. Evidence and witnesses are generally presented before **NCLT** for taking the decisions and **NCLAT** generally reviews decisions of **NCLT** and checks it on a point of law or fact.

The scenario changed here Mr Cyrus at every stage, Mistry positioned himself as the victim, championing minority shareholder rights and seeking to overturn board decisions taken after his ouster, including one that converted Tata Sons into a private firm from public.

On 18 December order of the National Company Law Appellate Tribunal (NCLAT) reinstating ousted Tata Sons chairman Cyrus Mistry as chairman comes as a major embarrassment for Mr Ratan Tata at the far end of his illustrious career.

What Is Expected?

The acrimonious battle between Mistry and Tata was one of the worst boardroom battles India Inc has seen, bringing to the fore such questions as the powers of promoters in summarily removing top executives (in this case, without adequately explaining the reasons upfront, but later alleging non-performance), the extent of powers of retired, larger-than-life executives (such as Tata) in the running of the day-to-day matters of a group they were once associated with, issues related to corporate governance, and the power of minority shareholders vis-a-vis majority shareholders. A lot of these issues are likely to be debated again in the apex court if Tata plans to take the matter there. The stakes are high in this battle for control of a group with over $110 billion (Rs 7.8 lakh crore) in revenues, 29 listed companies under its belt, operations in 160 countries, and employing over 660,000 people.

The NCLAT's verdict on Wednesday in the ongoing Tata-Mistry saga is likely to have far-reaching impact on other holding companies in India since the tribunal's judgement attempts to offer more say to minority shareholders in both listed and unlisted holding firms, many of which are run by family trusts of their promoters.

If the NCLAT decision on Article 75 of the Articles of Association (AoA) of Tata Sons Ltd is upheld by the Supreme Court, unlisted holding companies will neither be able to misuse the powers of the majority share-holders nor can they abruptly convert the status of a company from public to private or vice versa, both of which will benefit minority shareholders.

Article 75 gives Tata Sons the power to ask any shareholder to sell their holdings by passing a special resolution, a rule that can be potentially used to force Mistry family firms to exit Tata group at any moment. The shares can, however, only be sold to other existing shareholders, or outsiders chosen by the board. The board also decides the fair value of the shares as per the AoA.

The NCLAT also found that Tata Sons converted from a public company to a private entity without requisite approvals, which was illegal and ordered that it be reversed.

Public companies attract higher corporate governance standards, compared to a private company under the company's law. The appellate's decision to prohibit Tata Sons from conversion will ensure that minority shareholders in every unlisted public company are treated more fairly.

Conclusions

The decision of NCLAT shall forever change the corporate governance pattern and it shall make the promoters to have high moral and ethical values rather than act in a haphazard manner. The minority shareholders shall also get importance in the organizations rather than just to remain puppet stakeholders before the majority. It shall also encourage wide base of investors to come forward and invest in the corporate sector.

Case Questions

1. Is Tata and sons justified in the first place to act in the manner done by them against Mr Cyrus?

2. Is there a need to amend the companies act to accommodate so that article 75 is not misused by the majority shareholders to their benefit?

5

'AI and the Ethical Dilemma'

A Case Study on the Impact of AI on Business and Social Ethical Values

Learning Objectives

The digitalization of business processes has definite impact on the way business process was conducted so far especially on reduced human interactions and replacement by AI-driven systems like machine learning, block chains for Industry 4.0 lack of empathy, feelings, and teamwork facilitations and advantages.

Majority interactions between employees are like answering MCQs rather than discussions and deliberations on issues concerning on the job work environment.

This has also resulted in Work From Home (WFH) interactions through emails and Webinars on online platforms affecting the normal health of the executives and associates and also resulting in lack of freedom from monotony lack of social interactions which so very essential for overall well-being of people and society in general.

Each and everyone in this situation has to find out better ways for disallowing melancholy and frustration around.

This case study deals on specific topics and situations in which one needs to experience and lookout for ways to avoid feeling worthless when dominated by AI-driven businesses processes.

Synopsis

Artificial Intelligence (AI) is widely misunderstood and still too rudimentary for us to be worrying. But it is not soon to contemplate the

Indian Business Case Studies. Roopa Praveen, Dilip Aher, and Nilesh Anute, Oxford University Press. © ASM Group of Institutes, Pune, India 2022. DOI: 10.1093/oso/9780192869418.003.0005

ethical implications if Intelligent Machines (ML) and Systems (IoT) AI has the potential to be a transformative as advent of electricity to the world by transforming the entire aspects of dealing and interacting with data which eventually would reduce human interphase on a mega scale. There will be more machines connected with machines than human interactions at the organizational level. Is this only a hype? Far from reality? Is the phrase AI is it a misnomer? Since we know that human intelligence and the spirit has much more influence than the Bits and Bytes? Can human consciousness be uploaded on a cloud or duplicated with computer algorithms?

The Reality

There are predictions that AI will enable machines to have human-like feelings and emotions. Could this be possible can we imagine the situation where in acute human emotions such as love-hate and compassions can be coded and enacted by robots? But we as human beings are gullible after all. Can you believe that more than 1 million humans have asked their Alexas to marry them in 2017 alone (Amazon).

Today already AI systems are up to do their best to replicate functions of human beings in their brain functions although the scale of emulations is very limited in spite of deep learning techniques. Herein lies the problem though an AI system is as good as the quality and content of the data it receives it is able to interpret within the confines of available context. The computer does not understand what it has analysed so it is unable to apply its analysis to other scenarios since it cannot distinguish between causation and correlation.

AI however works very well in performing tasks that match patterns it is conversant with in the form and pattern of data fed to its systems to obtain objective outcomes. It cannot be subjective to situations outside the coded patterns. It can include playing chess driving a car and in identifying cancer lesions in a mammogram perhaps. These systems can be incredibly helpful and accurate than human investigations since there are many but limited moves and patterns in the tasks to be handled. Of course with more accurate data the systems will keep on improving.

Although an AI machine could do a better job than a radiologist in spotting cancer it will not be able to replicate the wisdom and the perspectives of a radiologist. It won't be able to empathize with a patient in the way a doctor can do. This is where an AI presents a risky situation of which we need to worry about since AI operates on objective measurements and judgements. Such outcomes at times could be scary and influence the reflective responses and depressive, scary reactions in the patients and his/her relatives and highly susceptible to human biases.

Issues such as granting a loan and admitting a student to a college or university or keeping the parent away from its parents/children/siblings for likely impacts purely based on objective investigative interventions through AI-enabled equipment which could at time be detrimental to someone's life.

AI throws up many ethical dilemmas around as to how we use the technology. It has already proven its utility in designing and using machines to kill enemies in the battlefield with drones which can even recognize faces and provide attack commands to the controls. China is already using AI to allocate codes—social credits to set of people based on behaviours. In the US the AI-enabled equipments can differentiate and identify people from Whites to African Americans and provide selective data for evaluation of population intensity propensity, etc. AI Machines enable gender-based segregations for allocations of social benefits based on gender inequality.

The complex situations created by social media apps such as Fb, YouTube are less said about is better creating filter bubbles and hotbed of misinformation and fakes. Technology obviously is opening up new frontiers but it is also presenting new challenges the world must confront/ More than ever before we need to exercise wisdom on all aspects of new technologies-from design to deployment with fake news and deep fakes there are too many confusing signals around facts which make the role of a commoner or stakeholder in the analyses and dissemination of information very challenging.

It is very difficult to differentiate between truth and opinions, preferences, and at times blatant lies. Privacy has become more ephemeral and almost unaffordable sophisticated data mining and facial recognition tolls and techniques enabled through AI are the very threats to privacy and personal data secrecy and security.

We are already witnessing identifying and location of targets for surgical strikes. Mind well Alexa and SIRI are constantly access our interactions and conversations for commercial exploitations not only for present generations but also for future generations yet to arrive this may help authorities in deciding the policies and prices but definitely fosters discrepancy in the access and exploitation during the digital world.

AI has given rise to technologies that help humans and animals to live longer and healthier free of major genetical disorders but will these things ensure a better quality of life? Living for say more than 100 years does not guarantee more meaningful and joyful life. The technology alone does not enable flourishing and meaningful life in spite of the fact that today more than ever before people are connected across the globe through social media loneliness is one single pervasive ghost and has reached epidemical proportions.

Technology cannot enable meaningful and deeper connections that promote empathy and kindness. Providing robot-assisted living is on the other hand is precipitating suicidal tendencies amongst ageing societies.

Similarly robot assisted teaching tools are deprived of personal touch between the teacher and the taught resulting in diminished creative thinking and critical thinking more focused on how to get the degrees enabling eligibility for degrees without debates and discussions. Ones personality including personal hygiene and discipline, including attitudes and interpersonal behaviours often times taking the back seat.

We are eager to design and develop machines which closely resemble human beings and paradoxically treating human beings more as machines. What does it mean to be a human in the AI age? How should humans relate to machines?

The Machines do not seek the kind of emotional and relational reciprocities which humans and animals do. Will AI be intended to shape human relational interactions and emotions? Humans are more used to face challenges and struggle to achieve acceptance in mutual interactions.

The concept of internet of bodies (Human/Animals) Iob as similar to IoT with a chip implanted in human bodies is the current buzzword. With a totally revamped way of life with telepresence, remote intimacy technologies or teledildonics. Technology serves the best when it helps to do things which humans aren't capable of but it might be catastrophic if it starts replacing human beings in the most personal and empathetic relationships.

Generationally we have had the luxury of learning by mistakes and course corrections. However when mistakes are likely to influence huge number of members of the society the cost of learning becomes prohibitive in the age of rapid changes. Technology is changing exponentially at much higher speeds which while helping us avoid the mistakes may also impede sustainability of the planet and space. The fossil fuel story, the use of plastics, and now the batteries may land us in major environmental issues in future hence it may be prudent to embed self-regulatory corrective (warning systems) to avoid retreating our steps for sustainability and survival as we progress.

Rather than focusing heavily on super intelligence we need to focus on ethical issues about how we should be using these technologies and the essential does and do nots.

Case Questions

1. The current generation is caught up in the hurricane of technological changes clubbed in as AI-enabled technology and techniques, unnerving and challenging the basics of ethical beliefs and systems and in spite of demonstrative effects of climate change and catastrophic effects of nuclear energy endangering human life we are apparently engaged in treading similar path of self-destruction again under the garb of AI dominated way of life.

2. What are the compelling reasons for the global leaders to adopt such technologies? Is it merely commercial aspects? Which are driving these issues? What happens if we take a pause?

3. AI Technology is out to nullify the human element in our enterprises rendering major chunk of our society as unemployable is this not a warning bell to question the basic objectives technology-driven initiatives? Who takes up the consequential responsibility?

6

'Intense Fear Syndrome of Potential Job Loss'

A Case Study on Issues of Working Professionals in India's IT Sector

Learning Objectives

At times after having been in a steady employment in a reputed IT sector company it comes as a shocker to know that the sector which held one of best employer status not far ago has all of a sudden started shedding its manpower base by resorting to Pink Slips for disengagement of employees without any rhyme or reason but just on the pretext of redundancy and overstaffing.

The employees on the other hand having enjoyed the privilege of working for an IT industry in spite of strenuous workload and indifferent work timings were happy to be leading above average lifestyles with adequate social recognition.

The start of this employee cropping process as applied by major IT sector industry including the leaders, nonconforming to any of the existing regulation protecting employment has created a near chaos amongst both young and senior executives in IT sector. By a similar rational that the IT sector employs highly educated and trained manpower the sector had disallowed any attempts to give its employees any powers to form any unions or associations to record and resist such draconian moves of simply giving 'Pink Slips' for severing employment many executives.

This case study attempts to explain the current situation in the IT sector employees and analyses few ways in which both the management and employees could resolve the crisis.

Indian Business Case Studies. Roopa Praveen, Dilip Aher, and Nilesh Anute, Oxford University Press. © ASM Group of Institutes, Pune, India 2022. DOI: 10.1093/oso/9780192869418.003.0006

Case Details

IT sector is facing serious issues of downsizing of manpower employers just send mail to employees mentioning 'With deep regret, we inform you that … your continued employment is not warranted. We would be relieving you from your employment from the 30th day of this letter.'

This phenomenon of issuing 'pink slip' is common in sector including professionals working for IT giant Tata Consultancy Services (TCS) recently, of retrenching more than three lacs employees, resulted in creating as urge among employees to form a union.

Bharathi Dasan, a Chennai based Form for IT Employees (FITE), said that TCS is now on a drive to lay off more than 25,000 IT employees whose has 8–20 years experience in the company. They are also planning to replace these experienced employees with fresh hands, whereby they get an estimated saving of Rs. 80,000 crores, as fresh employees expectations are very less. He further said that TCS has given notice to around 4,000 employees so far.

Lay off senior level in technical have been predicted by Experis IT Employment Outlook Survey from Experis IT-Manpower Group India for October 2017–March 2018. In the survey only 3% of employers need senior-level people in IT sector. The highest demand is for candidates having 0–5 years experience and 41% demand is for middle-level employees, i.e., 5–10 years experience.

Science graduates have top opportunities in top IT sector industries. As the years passed on, these people became managers and lost their basic technical skills. Now the new challenge is to re-skilling re-booting these middle-level workforces, to keep pace with the rapid changes. The top management people meet people in the outside world. The junior staff are earlier lot to learn new technologies. Thus the middle-level managers are considered as the weakest link in the chain and they are difficult to change. IT industries are worried about middle-level engineers, who lost touch with coding abilities and have not updated their tech skill sets.

In a research by Japanese brokerage firm Nomura, in a research note, said that the job cuts of 2–3% of nearly 7,60,000 by Infosys, Cognizant, Tech Mahindra, and Wipro are not material.

Industrial growth is from $100 million in 1992 to $146 billion last year. However, the role of middle-level managers is confusing due to their inability to adapt to new jobs in IT domain where technology changes very rapidly.

For their own survival, middle-level managers should try to change themselves with the changing environment and update their technical skills.

Middle-level management problem came to surface when TCS announced its intention to reduce 1–2% of its workforce, who are mostly engineers having more than 10 years experience. IT management feels that middle management managers are not updating their technological skills.

These middle-level managers, who do not have any option but to move out of their companies may find it difficult to grab a new job as the technical knowledge they have became obsolete with the change of time. Hence, IT firms may come out with new strategies of skill training in future.

As per the times job survey carried out of 755 HR Managers, 68% of respondents observed skill gap in middle management, 44% felt that the skill gap has widened during last three years; 32% did not feel any skill gap; another 32% felt it has diminished. Only 24% felt that the skill gap is the same.

Three are two major trends in IT sector. One, that of AI and machine learning. Second, legacy skill-sets going out of date. Therefore, there is risk to jobs due to these trends. The good news is that huge number of jobs are created in IT sector.

Artificial intelligence (AI) is an integral part of digitalization. IT industry is collecting, analysing, and managing data which result into creation of intelligent machines and computer programmes, which is programmed to find solutions to problems. AI increases productivity to a great extent, cut costs. According to research Statista, worldwide AI revenue should increase by a CAGR 2016–2025E of around 57% to USD 36.8 bn. Autonomous vehicles, speech recognition, and natural language processing are currently in focus with products such as Amazon's Alexa or Google's home assistant gaining immense popularity.

Capgemini is using IBM's cognitive consulting tool Watson to assign people to projects, while Infosys is building a machine learning platform that will help project managers take proper decisions as to number of people required for a project as well as the timeline for completion.

Simplilearn, a digital training company, highlights that 'digital domains such as Big Data, Artificial Intelligence, Internet of Things (IOT), Cloud Computing and Cyber Security' are the new job roles that will dominate the IT workforce.

Therefore, IT companies fight to retain their top talent. They are not ready to shell out increment for mid-level managers. Tech Mahindra has kept the salary revision of employees in abeyance for more than six years till further notice.

Pink slips may be served to employees who are in testing, technology support, and system administration since these will be managed by AI and robotics automation-based systems.

Ideally it is not fair for an employer to tell the employee to leave just because his performance is not up to the mark. Generally I.T. firms give number of chances for employees to improve their performance.

It is felt that management should take maximum initiative in the area of learning and development to help employees to become good leaders. Middle-level management staff needs more attention so that they do not become redundant in their skills. Top leaders should also be developed and motivated to the maximum extent to become the best leaders who have the capability to achieve the challenging management targets.

Employee Anxieties

An IT engineer who lost the job said that in the last six months he got more grey hair than he had in the last five years and he feared that he would lose his opportunities in IT market, if he revealed his identity.

Another person of 46 years was asked to resign from IT company at Pune in February last year after serving there for six years. In fact, he headed a team of six people and was evaluated as 'best performer' for five consecutive years. He planned to buy a branded car at the end of the year after getting a promotion. His 20 years career crashed down in February last year, as he was asked to resign with immediate effect. He was jobless since then.

Thousands of IT middle-aged men and women in India are facing same survival crisis.

Another IT engineer called Anil was suddenly removed from a project and asked to leave.

Another 36-year-old, who was laid off after 15 years of experience in Europe and America, commented that his removal was unethical and criminal without giving him any explanation. He failed to understand where he had erred for his sudden removal.

The phenomenon is removal of staff is happening in Pune, Bangalore, Hyderabad, and Chennai, the major IT hubs of India.

IT professionals in Pune came together and formed the Forum for IT Employees (FITE) in various cities in India. Every weekend they meet and discuss their strategies to fight the cases. This group consists of employees from almost all IT companies. However, they do not want their identity to be known to public fearing loss of job.

Many employees feel that IT companies do not specify what skills are required by them when they face delivery pressures. This is almost same as the problems faced in US manufacturing companies in the 1980s when automation emerged in manufacturing sector.

An I.T professional from Pune committed suicide by jumping from terrace and in his suicide note he had written that in IT there is no job security. Employees are worried a lot about their families.

It is reported that about 1,00,000 IT employees lost job in different parts of the country in the last one year.

Prakash Mahalingam, a 32-year-old techie working in a software company commented that about 6,00,000 people from IT sector may lose job in a very short period. He is also afraid of his own job security. He feels that 40% of the workforce will become redundant due to automation.

Management's Points of View

According to Aruna Jayanthi, CEO of Capgemini India, the IT industry has problem in the middle management and if they have to work out on that area.

According to Noshir Kaka, M.D, McKinsey India, if 30% of engineers do not re-skill themselves they will be redundant. According to Peter Bendor Samuel, CEO of IT consulting firm Everest Group, freshers are added every year in IT sector to keep cost low and this results in excess of experienced employees. As per Rituparna Chakraborty, Team Lease Services Executive Vice President and Co-Founder, this is a situation where available talent did not keep pace at which industry was evolving and many may become redundant.

As per Global Hunt MD Sunil Goel this rationalization would happen in every 3–5 years in industry through new-age technologies and we have more impact now due to changed policies of US for foreign IT workers. He further added that this trend would continue for the next 1–2 years; and this give an opportunity for IT professionals to upgrade themselves and get new-age technologies where demand is going to be huge.

Infosys also has mentioned that they have plans to go for automation and artificial intelligence, besides the newer technologies. As per Saurabh Govil, Chief HR Officer, Wipro, they would be moving to shift 4,500 engineers into different projects. They can be re-skilled into newer technologies.

As per Sanford Bernstein, IBM is going to lay off 14,000 employees as they are surplus due to automation. Other IT and BPO multinationals, also would fall in line.

According to Siddarth Bharwani, Vice President of Jetking Infotrain, expected shockwaves in middle management level and these employees will have to undergo re-skilling to retain their jobs. As per IT management there is lot of pressure from clients to reduce the cost by 30%, otherwise they are not interested. Automation is the only way to achieve this.

Consultants/Media Views

Jayan said that the work culture in IT sector is such that management does not have time and attitude for networking. Hence they sack employees whenever they find that their performance is poor. Since they do not want others to know that their competency is low, they put in their papers silently.

Consultants feel that employees with less than a year's experience are better at office rather than employees with five years of experience because the newer employees are coming up with better technology solutions. Some other consultants feel that it is the greed and cost-cutting that motivates the IT management to take this type of inhuman steps.

Economist Arun Kumar told Arab News that the Indian government is not in a position to do much. Arvind Subramanian (Adviser to Prime Minister Narendra Modi) of the website of New Delhi Television (NDTV), showed concern over anti-globalization tendencies, expressed in the last US election which affects Indian jobs.

As per Kamall Karanth, MD, Kelly Services & KellyOCG India, automation will not take away jobs because for managing automation like Robot we still need people. It is felt that automation will make irrelevant another 80% reduction in man manpower in 2018. Tech analyst feel that this will affect 65% of the global IT off-shored work and 40% of business process hiring in India.

Automation is accelerating its speed due to the client's compulsion to embrace automation to increase quality and productivity and timely delivery. There is pressure from overseas vendors to invest on automation tools like AI and Robotics.

As per the World Bank statistics, automation took away 69% of jobs in India.

As per Experis IT Manpower Group India, layoffs in IT sector in India is likely to continue for another 6–12 months. It is estimated that $155 billion IT sector employs around 3.9 million people in India and half of the existing workforce will be irrelevant unless they have updated their skills as per the market needs.

As per R. Chandrashekhar, President NASSCOM, re-skilling is the buzzword in IT sector and hence employees should either re-skill or perish. Hence about 3 lakhs people may lose the jobs in coming three years. IT companies like Cognizant opt for voluntary separation packages for various levels of their employees.

However, there is a silver line in dark cloud. There are promising opportunities and open ups where digitalization and automation will create newer career opportunities for IT professionals. These new technologies can improve the performance substantially. Hence, employees will have to enhance their skills in use of robotics, machine learning, and AI.

As per Indian Brand and Equity Foundation, the IT industry employs around 10 million people. NASSCom (The National Association of Software and Services Companies) said that the contribution of IT sector is 7% of India's GDP (Gross Domestic Products). The crisis faced by IT sector is the question of survival of both employers and employees.

Case Questions

1. What are the problems faced by middle management staff members at IT Sector in India from various angles?

2. IT contribution in Indian GDP is 7%. How far the current layoff at Indian IT sector is going to affect the Indian economy and what are its possible solutions?

3. Explain redundancy of job and its relationship with automation w.r.t. IT sector in India.

SECTION II
CASE STUDIES IN FINANCE MANAGEMENT

Financial Accounting, Direct/Indirect Taxation, Banking and Insurance

7

Punjab and Maharashtra Cooperative Bank Scam

(PMC Bank)

A Case Study in Coercive Financial Scam

Learning Objectives

Financial scams perpetrated by the banking system is not a new thing for most of us since the world over there have been more scams committed by major banks by corrupting the very purpose for which the banks and the banking systems are designed. The main culprit in majority of such scams is the essential reward systems and performance evaluation of the banking chiefs is implemented. The sheer competition for survival amidst neck-breaking competition to rollover funds to profits leads to severe greed and crucification of core values by the senior executives. And the manipulative customer knows how exactly the banks are obliged to extend loans and highly flexible repayment schedules available to him for avoiding repayments.

The stricter the actions initiated the more the tendency to push such unrecoverable loans below the carpet by the CEOs of the bank who in the way are coercing the system to bend backwards at the cost of the banks financial health and leading to insolvency and loss of depositors money.

This case helps understanding one such debacle and scam at a well-known bank in India.

Indian Business Case Studies. Roopa Praveen, Dilip Aher, and Nilesh Anute, Oxford University Press. © ASM Group of Institutes, Pune, India 2022. DOI: 10.1093/oso/9780192869418.003.0007

Case Details

The bank started its operations in a small room at Sion on 13 February 1984. In 1999 the all India bank depositors association felicitated the bank for the work ethics oriented to depositors' service. Within a period of six years the bank bagged the status of scheduled bank; as in 2000 the RBI conferred scheduled status to P&M cooperative bank.

The bank is the youngest bank to achieve the scheduled bank status. Another milestone in its progress path was the multi-state status, which the bank was conferred in 2004 providing the bank with the national exposure. Nine times the bank has been awarded the title of Best Urban cooperative bank by Maharashtra state cooperative banks' association. It has also been awarded by NPCI for the lowest dispute ratio in cooperative banking sector.

The bank was the pioneer to mention payee name in passbook, the same system being followed by other banks as per RBI guidelines. The bank implemented its belief in women empowerment by having 70% women employees and by giving preferential treatment for education loan to girls/women.

Under the corporate social responsibility, the bank has acquired three banks for cooperative sector from 2008 to 2010. In a span of 35 years the bank has spread 137 branches across six states. A profitable cooperative bank which booked Rs. 99.69 crore profit in financial year 2019.

The Scam

With this glorious and successful history of the bank, people have never ever expected any inefficiency in the bank; hence the HDIL P&MC bank scam was shocking news for people in banking fraternity and the depositors of the bank.

It all started when a few of women employees of the bank have suspected some irregularities in functioning and found some ghost accounts. On 23 September the central bank imposed operational restrictions on PMC bank for six months; on realization of gross misconduct in loan disbursement and management. On 24 September 2019, RBI issued directions under section 35A and section 56 of the banking regulation act 1949.

The crux of the fraud is that the top management officials have given huge loan to the HDIL (Housing Development and Infrastructure Ltd.) and its associated companies. The amount sanctioned was as huge as it was 70% of the total loan disbursements by the bank. The total amount of fraud was said to be Rs. 4355 crore, which led to shooting up of the NPA of the bank to 73%.

The PMC bank has allegedly favoured the promoters of HDIL by allowing them to operate password-protected 'masked accounts'. In order to safeguard the interest of the HDIL, and to hide the discrepancies and misappropriation, around 21,049 bogus/fake bank accounts were opened to conceal 44 loan accounts which had turned into NPA.

The bank's software was also tampered to conceal these loan accounts. Just before the scam has been brought to light, the 50 crore. Loan was disbursed to HDIL on 30 August 2019 to utilize it for repayment of a loan taken from Bank of India by HDIL and its group companies. The total amount outstanding; constituting interest plus principal amount, from HDIL and its associates was around Rs. 6117.93 crore as on 31 August 2019.

The Enforcement Directorate (ED) has sealed the assets of Rs. 3500 crore of HDIL group and HDIL Chief Rakesh Wadhawan and his son Sarang Wadhawan have been arrested by Mumbai police as accused of omitting a fraud on PMC bank.

The Bombay high court has appointed a three members committee to oversee the sale of assets of HDIL. A litigation was filed in public interest by advocate Sarosh Damania and Economic Offense Wing (EOW). The liability to the bank as per the FIR lodged by EOW was Rs 4355 crore.

Former PMC bank MD has admitted the hoodwinking the auditors, bank's board and RBI years together by concealing the default on loan. In a letter of explanation given by Thomas to RBI the reason behind concealing the facts was to safeguard the reputation of HDIL and of the bank. According to him, HDIL was the major customer of the bank with good track record of servicing the loan since 1990. HDIL came to rescue the bank in 1986–1987 when the bank had come on the verge of closure due to some unlawful deeds of some of the borrowers.

The company infused capital and saved the bank. In 2004, the group rescued bank from cash crunch by depositing Rs. 100 crore to help the bank. Further he added that if the loan to HDIL asset being turned as NPA then they might not be able to book the interest on these accounts, resulting into hampering financial position of the bank.

As the loan amount was huge, declaring it as NPA would have affected the profitability of the bank and with a fear of facing a regulatory action by RBI. The bank continued to report all accounts as standard assets. It was not brought to the notice of the board.

Statutory auditors were checking only incremental advances and not the entire operations in all the accounts this helped the culprits to conceal the stressed accounts by replacing them with dummy accounts. As the loans were mentioned as loans against deposits and were of small amounts, they were never checked and questioned by RBI.

During the investigation it has been revealed that during 2008, HDIL entered into various new business ventures like acquisition of fields in Jordon, hotels, and media ventures, etc. There were huge cross-holdings in the companies, creating a maze of complex holdings.

The investigation by ED revealed that on various accounts of HDIL group, overdraft facilities were pending since 2013–2014, but the accounts were further enhanced in 2019 with additional overdraft facility by projecting it as enhancing of OD limit. This was done to prevent the account being declared as NPA.

In the financial year 2018–2019 the bank saw increase in stressed assets which affected its financial position. The asset quality of the bank declined as the NPA ratio to gross advances increased to 3.76% from the earlier one of 1.99%. To cleanse the balance sheet the bank sold NPA portfolio to CFM asset reconstruction Pvt. Ltd. for Rs. 105 crore as of March 2019.

Effect of the Scam/Reparations of the Scam

On 23 September 2019 RBI imposed operational restrictions on the bank; this resulted into restriction of withdrawals by the depositors.

Joy Thomas the MD of the bank was suspended and the MD and his son were arrested along with other few officials of HDIL and of the bank.

Case Questions

1. In your opinion do the auditors and the central bank officials also responsible for their mass negligence towards the misappropriations?

2. What safeguard points would have been implemented to avoid such frauds and safeguard the depositors' hard-earned money?

3. What precautionary measure one can take as a depositor to safeguard his money?

8

The Monster of Non-Productive Assets

A Case Study on Mounting NPA

Learning Objectives

As students and faculty of management studies in finance management need to know the essential features of company balance sheets, their purpose, contents and specifics areas of assets and liabilities of an organization to ultimately understand the financial health of the company this case study tries to expose few of the lacunae which have crept in to the balance sheets basically hide or misrepresent certain financial transactions to avoid the eagle's eyed investigative studies by the external auditors and to hoodwink the prospective and current investors to make believe that the company is good financial health through manipulating the data.

This case study is one such example wherein financial fraudulent entries are made in the balance sheet.

The reader also understands as to how to read the balance sheet and look for such fraudulent practices to avoid manipulative practices in company balance sheets.

Synopsis

Balance sheets as per norms have to reveal true positions of the business. Question is do balance sheets of banks do this? Unfortunately they do not. Accounts are shown in assets side but they are not so and are classified as non-performing so what made them to non-perform and what are its effects.?

The move on the part of the government to inject capital of Rs 2.11 lakh crore into public sector banks (PSBs) gives strength to the above fact.

Indian Business Case Studies. Roopa Praveen, Dilip Aher, and Nilesh Anute, Oxford University Press. © ASM Group of Institutes, Pune, India 2022. DOI: 10.1093/oso/9780192869418.003.0008

Why this has to be done and is this enough is the question. In making this move, there was an implied acceptance that the recovery process set up through the Insolvency and Bankruptcy Code (IBC) reform had not been working at the desired pace. When the Reserve Bank of India asked PSBs to work on the recovery process for 12 large exposures which account for 50% of the total non-performing assets (NPAs) worth ₹8 lakh crore in the banking system, it was expected that by December 2017, the banks would recover about Rs 2 lakh crore. But it's already November and we know that recovery is eluding us and the process may take longer. Till then the banking system will starve for capital.

According to RBI October to December report, the gross NPAs of PSB are just under Rs. 4 lakh crore, and they collectively account for 90% of such rotten apples in the country's banking portfolio. In terms of net NPAs, their share is even higher—at 92% of the total bad loans reported so far in the banking system.

What Is NPA?

- The assets of the banks which don't perform (that is, don't bring any return) are called NPA or bad loans. Bank's assets are the loans and advances given to customers. If customers don't pay either interest or part of principal or both, the loan turns into bad loan.
- According to RBI, terms loans on which interest or instalment of principal remain overdue for a period of more than 90 days from the end of a particular quarter is called an NPA.
- However, in terms of Agriculture/Farm Loans, the NPA is defined as under—for short duration crop agriculture loans such as paddy, Jowar, Bajra, etc., if the loan (instalment/interest) is not paid for two crop seasons, it would be termed as an NPA. For long duration crops, the above would be one crop season from the due date.

The Case Background

Banking industry is in bad shape in the country where the capital is becoming insufficient to meet the growing demands. The reason is rise in

NPA's due to which if calculated properly almost all the PSB have to shut down the shop. Basel accord has prescribed capital norms but the bank's position is far from reality. The government has taken decision to induce funds but in reality the funds are nowhere sufficient for banks to come out of the red. Why has this situation arisen and which sectors are contributing for the same?

How Grim Is the Situation?

- According to the RBI's statistical tables relating to banks in India 2015–2016, NPAs were 3% of gross advances of all banks in India in 2013.
- By 2016, they had grown to 9.3%. The increase was much more pronounced for nationalized banks—from 2.9% in 2013 to 13.8% in 2016—compared to privately owned banks where the NPAs rose from 2% of gross advances in 2013 to 3.1% in 2016.
- For the 10 worst PSBs, gross NPAs averaged 16.4% of gross advances as on December 2016, from 22.4% for the Indian Overseas Bank to 14.1% for the Central Bank of India—in effect, each having thoroughly destroyed its balance sheet.
- The system does not have enough capital to take care of its bad loans.

What Possibly Led to This Situation?

- In an exuberant milieu that started with the UPA 1 government and continued until three years after the global financial crisis of 2008, large corporations conceived major projects proposals in capital-intensive sectors such as power, ports, airports, housing, and highway construction.
- Banks were only too keen to lend, often without sufficient evaluation of risks and returns.
- Things started worsening with the policy paralysis brought about by the spectrum and coal mining scandals.
- Soon, most projects were getting stuck, especially in power and highways; and banks found their loans going sour.

• Initially, the extent of NPAs was hidden by 'ever-greening'. They were revealed as the RBI tightened the norms.

The Path Followed

It is significant that capital is being infused into banks. This could give the banking system a good breathing time to enhance its credit portfolio and restore value out of the NPA accounts. We may have to watch the situation unfolding over the next three years. During this time, the regulator, banks, and the government will have to focus on the quality of public sector banking assets, the NPAs, and the recovery. There has been a broad-brush approach to the quality assessment. The system will have to conduct more analysis, more evaluation sector-wise in terms of its potential for value restoration and enhancement. They will have to understand which sector is in a position to restore more economic value in six to eight quarters. Some sectors may perhaps take longer.

The last thing the economy and the banking system can afford is a further drop in economic value. What may be perceived as Rs 8 lakh crore problems today might grow into a much larger amount. The quality of governance will play a significant role in this regard. There has not been any worthwhile effort on this unfortunately. There will have to be more reforms to put a higher order of governance in the banking sector. Ensuring performing boards at public-sector banks do become more critical. The last point which is equally important is that as long as the government wants to hold on to 51% equity in PSBs we cannot have periodic injection by way of recaps bonds.

To fund the economy, the government will have to make a yearly budgetary allocation of the amount of capital required by PSBs. Programmes such as Indradhanush and small budgetary allocations will not work. The PSBs need budgetary allocation of at least ₹75,000–80,000 crore each year.

The announcement of a stimulus into PSBs has been apparently understood as a bounty for the banks. An atmosphere is being projected that the government has been too generous to the banks and is serious about helping them to resolve the bad loans crisis. The quantum of capitalization announced leads one to believe so. In reality, this will not enable banks to recover the alarmingly huge bad loans which is the main issue confronting them.

Stressed Assets

The total stressed assets, bad loans, and restructured loans in banks are in the region of Rs 15 lakh crore. Instead of taking tough action on defaulters, the government came out with a 'novel scheme' to foist insolvency and bankruptcy proceedings on defaulters.

This measure is not going to result in the recovery of bad loans. That is why the RBI has asked PSBs to be prepared for a deep haircut, up to 50% of the dues. Recently, on one account, a bank managed to recover just 6% of the total loan amount of Rs 950 crore. On 12 accounts, the dues are Rs 2.5 lakh crore. One can only imagine the additional provisions banks will have to make this year. There are more skeletons in the cupboard.

The Reality

There is a rush to 'punish' corporate culprits. The fact is that this is not a punishment, rather it is a reward. The defaulter promoter can himself bid before the IBC proceedings. Obviously, he is likely to be the highest bidder. So, he will retain his company but will have to shell out less than what he borrowed. This is legal innovation to pay less. But in the bargain, banks will lose huge amounts. One can safely predict that all banks will be running into losses by the end of the current financial year. Last year, while the gross operating profits were Rs 1, 58,982 crore, after provisions for bad loans (Rs 1,70,370 crore), the net loss was Rs 11,388 crore.

This year, it is bound to be worse. The IBC is only a ploy to extend favours to big corporates to escape from their liability at the cost of the public exchequer. Now let us see whether the recap announced by the Finance Minister will help PSBs, labelled as inefficient and incompetent. If banks would have recovered these loans, their interest revenue would have been more; income levels higher, profits high and they would have generated capital internally out of the profit. That door is closed because banks cannot recover loans through the IBC route. Thus, the banks' capital gets eroded and the capital adequacy ratio (CAR) becomes adverse.

Effects of Inadequate Capital

If banks do not have adequate capital, they cannot lend. This would dampen the economy, which is already in the doldrums. Hence to bolster the economy, banks have to be advised to give more loans. To give more loans, more capital is essential. That is why the announcement on recapitalization.

In the last three years, banks have written off ₹188,287 crore. We have to bear in mind that when banks lose money or when the government recapitalizes PSBs, it is all people's money and out of public savings kept in trust in the banks. People's money should be for people's welfare and not to fund corporate default or to recapitalize the banks to adjust these bad loans. The decision by the government to further capitalize PSB is a welcome move. But does it really solve the problem of the lack of capital adequacy of PSB? Let us examine.

Effects of NPA's

The problem of hidden bad assets is pervasive across the entire banking system. Both public and private sector banks are part of the story. If one bank had been undertaking fraudulent accounting practices and hiding problems, it could have been blamed, and its management punished, as in the case of Satyam and the conviction of Ramalinga Raju. If the problem was limited to PSB, we would have found solutions in their governance. Private Banks have also been hiding bad assets.

The present NPA crisis appears to be as much a failing of the banking regulator. For many years, despite its unquestioned powers to regulate, supervise, and inspect banks, the regulator did not take action against banks that were hiding their bad assets. Instead, it proposed one loan restructuring scheme after another. None of the schemes, like CDR, SDR, and S4A succeeded and stressed assets grew in number and value. It is only now, when credit growth has collapsed, that solving the problem cannot be postponed further and the regulator has become strict.

Regulatory failure across the world has led to changes in regulatory regimes, in laws and in institutions. Creating checks and balances is a necessary element of the reform process. Independence and accountability are two sides of the same coin. Regulators must have both.

Gross NPAs of Public and Private Sector Banks during 30 June 2016

S No.	Bank	Total Advances (Rs. in crore)	Gross NPA (Rs. in crore)	NPA Ratio (%)
1	Allahabad Bank	145,328	18,769	12.92
2	Andhra Bank	137,228	14,137	10.3
3	Bank of Baroda	269,115	35,604	13.23
4	Bank of India	274,391	43,935	16.01
5	Bank of Maharashtra	103,148	13,040	12.64
6	Bharatiya Mahila Bank Ltd.	627	3	0.4
7	Canara Bank	311,615	30,480	9.78
8	Central Bank of India	185,719	25,107	13.52
9	Corporation Bank	142,787	15,726	11.01
10	Dena Bank	81,114	9,636	11.88

Source: RBI; Parliament Questions Get the data Created with Data wrapper

Conclusions

In the discussions about the reform that should accompany recapitalization, it is important to remember that it is not enough to reform PSB. The problem of hiding NPAs is also present in private sector banks. The failures of banking regulation must be addressed and checks and balances created.

Case Questions

1. Majority of the NPAs are from the lending to few major groups of industries whose projects have either failed to take off or few them being in the gestation period for extending the initial projections. If the problems are so severe as to badly affect the cash flows in major financial institutions calling for bailout packages from the government. How do you expect to approach the problem in terms of turnaround strategy for the banking industry in India?

2. With demands of farmers to waive off loans in many Indian states of huge amounts running into lakhs of crores of rupees and the government having no alternative other than accepting these demands—Is NPA going to be a regular impediment to economic progress of India? Besides each and every loan recovery case of industry is getting in to NPAs and few of them resorting to running away from India to avoid punitive actions resulting in Government machinery getting occupied in bringing culprits to justice.

9

The Hindustan Bank Ltd

Synopsis

Specialization was a keyword till yesterday. The concept of management and aspects of management change every day with the introduction of new technology and thinking. The managers of today are not required only to be specialized in a particular field but also are expected to manage teams, i.e., HR, about the profitability and proper and cost-effective utilization of the financial resources, i.e., finance, trends in the market and consumer behaviour, i.e., marketing, the thrust of information technology in almost all areas of life, i.e., IT, knowledge of law, i.e., legal. Thus there is no escape for a manager if he wants to be a successful executive in a business scenario.

Banking is one of the very few industries, where one is required to use all these skills, irrespective of the cadre and the level of management where one is working, to give the best results.

The present case deals with this peculiar scenario mentioned above. We find so many banks going into liquidation, merger, or acquisition. The purpose behind all these measures is to make Indian banking scenario a force to be reckoned with, in the international market and curb the ill practices prevailing in the Indian banking field. The case takes into consideration various aspects of management. The case can be studied from various angles by using different skills of students of different specializations.

It is perceived by many that banking is nothing but finance and finance only. The myth is tried to be broken in this case. And hence this case is not meant only for the students of finance but all faculties of management can study this case from their point of view. The case though refers to a private banker, the principles are equally applicable in other situations and industries also.

Indian Business Case Studies. Roopa Praveen, Dilip Aher, and Nilesh Anute, Oxford University Press. © ASM Group of Institutes, Pune, India 2022. DOI: 10.1093/oso/9780192869418.003.0009

It has been observed that the word management sends wrong messages in the fora of managers. It really is painful to see that numerous managers to achieve results kill the management every day. Marketing has become selling, Human Resource has become manipulation of human beings, finance has become portraying fictitious results, Information Technology has become a separate world of few people, and above all the knowledge of Law has been utilized to prolong and deny the just and reasonable claims. However, the scene is not so depressing. There are numerous examples who have applied management in right sense and shown excellent results.

The Case Details

'It was quite a marathon meeting,' the CEO of Hindustan Bank told his deputy. 'It was really tiring, I must say,' replied the Dy. CEO.

'And I can't understand, why the GM Finance is so pessimistic about everything. I just don't like his approach.' 'Being a head of finance, he is too cautious, I feel.'

'He told me in the meeting that the accounts of M/S Apex Synthetics Pvt. Ltd were causing him concern. He almost suggested me that we were cheated in the deal of taking over the accounts of M/S Apex from Syndicate Bank. I knew the accounts were causing concern to Syndicate Bank. However, look at the assets of M/S Apex, total worth of all of them goes to the tune of Rs. 100 crores.'

'Perhaps, I feel, he wanted to bring to your notice certain hidden facts' 'Fool he is!' the CEO raised his hands in ex-asperation. 'Doesn't he know that though he is senior to me in age, I have more experience in credit and finance. And you know, we have made a clean profit of Rs. 9 crores. Government is planning to give subsidy to cotton industry to boost the export business.'

'Oh really! Then Apex will definitely prove to be a golden feather in our crown,' said the Dy. CEO.

'Moreover M/S Apex have promised to invest heavily in our forthcoming IPO. And moreover I know the family of the main promoter of the company very closely.' 'Thanks Sir. But our exposure of Rs. 24 crores to the group, including clean non-fund based facilities, is almost touching to the maximum of 5% of our Net Worth.' 'Oh yes! I know it. But we are not crossing the limit placed by RBI in any case. There will not be adverse remarks by RBI auditors. Any way, how are their Cash Credit account operations, do you have any idea?' 'No problem uptill now, barring few exceptions.'

'Well, it strengthens my assertion. I think we can have sound sleep,' the CEO laughed at his joke. The Dy. CEO left the cabin soon.

'This GM, Marketing is another silly cat.' The CEO muttered to himself. 'He does not take any decisions and sends all files to me for sanction. And to cap it all, he is least bothered about the profitability.' He remembered the way his talk went on in the meeting with the GM Marketing.

'Sir, our pet projects of Retail and Personal Banking Services branches and Commercial Banking Services Branches are going very well. The face lift of all the 8 branches is almost complete. However, the location of Zaveri Bazar and Kothrud branches need to be given a fresh thought,' said GM Marketing.

'Why? What is wrong in the present location?' asked CEO while sifting through the file in front of him.

'Our these branches are .5 kms away from the main banking bazaar, where most of the banks are located. There is no parking place and moreover these days customers deal with multiple banks. We are losing out the business.' 'How much business we have lost during last 12 months? Do you have the figures ready?'

'Well—we can get the figures if you want?' Next time come prepared and then argue. No point in wasting time over these matters. 'Sorry Sir And then this other matter of increasing the minimum balance of Savings accounts %>m Rs. 500/- to Rs. 5000/- in case of these branches. Kothrud is predominantly a pensioner's area and customers are not ready to keep so much balance in their Savings Accounts. As it is, with Rs. 500/- minimum balance, they are complaining. How about shifting branch to Karve Road.'

'Not a bad idea, but the road is totally packed and moreover it will be a very costly affair So let us remain where we are. We will have to market our products vigorously.'

But the costs are going to increase every year and we got to attend to this problem today or tomorrow. 'Agreed but I have to attend to the profitability of the Bank,' retorted the CEO. 'At least for the present, keep the problem in deep freezer.'

'Another area of concern is the delegation of authorities to the Managers of our branches. Our Delegated authorities have not been revised during past ten years. With the introduction of Personal and Commercial Branches, we ought to have fresh look at it so the managers of the branches will be well equipped to sanction bigger advances. Every small matter concerning marketing is referred to Head Office which increases workload of my department considerably.

This is just an idea, but I feel that if we establish a Regional Office, Northern Region, it will reduce our workload at least by 35%.' 'But we will require additional staff for that. And I don't think our Managers are capable of taking big business decisions? Sometimes 1 feel to change the whole lot!.' 'They need to be trained. And our Training Centre is very hard pressed and incapable of handling certain areas of modern day banking.'

'Well, that matter needs to be dealt by the H.R. Deptt. Any other matter of concern?' 'This is the last matter. We have lost the case of wrong return of cheque in the Pune District Forum. The forum has slapped Rs. 100,000/- as compensation on our face'. 'Let us go in appeal to State Forum.'

'But how about out of court settlement? The chances of winning are very slim?' 'Oh, forget it. We fight till the National Forum? Ask the advocate to delay the matter by about 4 to 5 years. The customer will be exasperated till then.'

'Really, these consumer forums are another headache' the CEO thought to himself. When he thought of headache, he thought immediately of General Manager, HRD. The General Manager always brings up topics of pain in the meetings. This time in the meeting he brought up topic of computerization of the bank which has rendered about 15% staff as flab.'

He had asked him very pointedly 'So what do you propose?' 'I have an idea that we may introduce Voluntary Retirement Scheme, in our Bank. Our s will be the first bank in private sector to offer VRS. Our average staff age is also between 40–45 years. If required, we may introduce young blood.' 'Our staff is our asset'. They have contributed in making our bank big in the private sector. I abhor the idea of throwing the staff when not found useful. See what has happened to Bank of India. They were the first to introduce the VRS in public sector. Their Chairman was very happy when he cut down the staff by 15% (10000 employees).

He even boasted of his success in the Banker's Club. And now they are repenting. Bank of India has lost cream of the intelligentsia. I don't want it to happen to us. Instead use our excess staff for the marketing and recovery purposes. Besides, this will be additional strain on our reserves and profitability. By the way have you prepared the list of clerical transfers? The union people will be coming tomorrow. 'Yes Sir, here it is.'

'Very good. As regards training, I have a different idea. How about employing outsiders for training our staff.'

'Outside Trainers have limitations. As far as banking is concerned, no outsider can be ideal than our own trainers. Instead, we may send our trainers to outside agencies for their development so that they train our own people as per our requirement.' 'O K. Go ahead with it. See that the cost is minimum and keep me informed about the programmes of the outsiders and performance of our Trainers.' The CEO had told him to go ahead, however, he was sure that the GM, HRD will come back to him with some other problem.

His phone rang. His P. A. was on the line 'Sir the G.M. Information Technology wants to meet you, shall I send him in?'

'O.K.', he said and put the receiver down.

The General Manager Information Technology cleared his throat. Looking at his papers he said, 'Sir, I have two matters to discuss. The first matter pertains to selection of software. We had asked quotations from Megasys and Flex. Magasys's total banking software FICLE is costlier than Flex's V-TUBE. The difference is about Rs. 2 crores. Besides, V-TUBE is not compatible for Indian Banking. Karwar Bank has filed a case against Flex as it does not suffice their needs. FICLE is compatible to Indian as well as Foreign Banking. However it is too bulky. I would suggest that we go for the FICLE.' 'Even, the MD of Karwar Bank told me that he was not very happy with Flex. Why don't you call Megasys for negotiations.'

'I already had a talk with them. They are not inclined for any discount.' 'Then for time being let us depend on our Internal software.'

'We are totally dependent on our in-house software. But for using UTI Bank's ATM (they use FICLE) by our customers is too costly and customers also have complained for additional charges levied by them.'

'Umm, Hold the situation for some more time. Let us see if Megasys comes down.' 'Second matter is training the staff members. If we decide to go for FICLE or V-TUBE, our staff members need to be trained on their Total Banking Solutions. It will take at least six months. Likewise, we will have to change all the cabling work which will at least take six months.'

'OK, when we decide about the software, we shall think about this.' 'Thank you Sir.'

Extract of Cash Credit Account of M/S Apex Synthetics Limit Sanctioned: Rs. 60 crores (Date taken over 1 June 2005) Primary Security: Hypothecation of cotton, cloth Stocks Drawing Power: Rs. 75 crores Margin 25% of stock cost.

Drawing Limit: Rs. 60 crores Stock statement frequency—Monthly

Date	Particulars Balance 2005	* Dr.	Cr.
01.09	To Bal. C/Fd	600000000	600000000
05.09	By J.K. Syn.	100000000	500000000
06.09	By Cash		50000004950000
			595000000
12.09	To DD Sri Mittals	100000000	595000000
18.09	By Cash		200000000395000000
21.09	To Processing Charges	150000	395150000
24.09	To Salaries	750000	395900000
26.09	To Quarterly Interest	5000000	400900000
01.10	To Kala Builders	55000000	455900000
04.10	To Excise By	2000000	45790000U
08.10	Arvind Mills		50000000552900000
06.10	To Arvind Mills	100000000	557900000
23.10	To Salaries	765000	553665000

Date	Particulars Balance 2005	* Dr.	Cr.
06.11	To Mittal Group	50000000	603665000
13.11	By Chougule		50000000553665000
18.11	To Ourselves	30000000	583665000
24.11	To Sal.	735000	584400000
		50000000	
08.12	To SAIL		634400000
18.12	By Mittal Irons		54400000580000000
26.12	To Quarterly Interest	32000000	612000000
2006	By Mittal Group		5200000560000000
05.1			
16.1	By Arvind Mill		60000000500000000
22.1	To ourselves	50000000	550000000
28.1	To Salaries	750000	550000000
05.2	To Sales Tax	750000	551000000
07.2	To Audit Fees	100000	551600000
26.2	To Salaries To	750000	552350000
08.3	J.K. Syn	50000000	602350000
24.3	To Quarterly Interest	37500000	639850000

Observations of RBI Auditors for accounts above Rs. 5 crores.

1. Drawing Limits not calculated properly and not checked by any officer
2. The statements of stock were not signed by proper authority
3. On the date of closing of the year many accounts were out of order
4. Ad-hoc limits sanctioned were not regularized within a period of 3 months
5. Stock statements not submitted as per stipulated frequency
6. Inspections not done as per stipulated frequency
7. Charge was not registered with registrar of companies
8. Modification of charge was not done in many cases

Profile of Hindustan Bank Pvt. Ltd.		
PERFORMANCE HIGHLIGHTS		
	(Rs. In crores)	
For the year	31 March 2006	31 March 2005
Total Income	504	502
Total Expenditure	388	363
Gross Profit	116	138
Operating Profit	70	62
Net Profit	70	62
Share Capital	41	41
Reserves	630	630
Current Deposits	401	460
Savings Deposits	1058	1045
Term Deposits	2575	1700
Secured Advances	3250	3111
Unsecured advances	113	98
Capital Adequacy (%)	15	12
Gross NP A (%)	8	9
Net NPA (%)	2	2
Branches (No.)	75	74
	(Extension counter merged)	(and 1 extension counter)
Employees	1778	1770

Conclusions

Nowadays management of banks smoothly amidst several responsibilities and limitations of the regulatory authorities has become a tight rope walk for the managers in the banking industry. Leading to over-cautious way of working and in the process of committing errors and defaults one needs to work under tremendous pressures of compliance and competition simultaneously. It is preferred that the rules are made a bit relaxed and permitting the bank executives as though they are managing a business unit both with competence and compliance.

Case Questions

1. How does a major bank today should update and train its senior executives in multi-tasking efforts and also deal with complex banking issues?

2. In view of severe competition up-gradation of operating systems in banking is becoming prohibitive. Manual operations are no more acceptable in the internet banking ecosystem What are the internet systems which could help driving traditional systems in AI climate?

SECTION III
MULTIDISCIPLINARY CASE STUDIES IN MARKETING, STRATEGY, OPERATIONS

Marketing Management, Strategic Management, Mergers and Acquisitions, and Operations Strategy

10

Leveraging China

A Case Study on Strategic Resource Leveraging

Learning Objectives

Study of Micromax's strategy of rebadging the handset and sailing them in the India market is important. Not only this the way the Micromax did the research of Indian consumers' demands is interesting in this. Also in 2011, Micromax shipped four million handsets worldwide in the second quarter. It's cornered 8% share in the home market, it's growth to 48% annually and continued selling 1.5 million phones every month in most of the countries, is very challenging to do a study on it. Another objective is to study the how and why phone market in India was pretty much a seller's market. Another objective is to study how it penetrated to Indian market by launching a phone with a 30-day power backup which was the necessity of Indian customers. It is also important to study how Micromax has given affordable handset price.

Synopsis

The simple strategy applied by the Micromax was to create high volumes, reach the customer base through effective distribution, give them products that are innovative and cost-effective. The Apple and Samsung lagged behind due to affordable handset price compared to Micromax with same features. Micromax launched handset as per their necessity of Indian market like 30-day power backup. Micromax orders 5,00,000 handsets at the entry-level from their contract manufacturers in China at one go. The order of 5,00,000 handsets volume is an example of growth in turn over and better cost. The appreciable thing of Micromax was it

Indian Business Case Studies. Roopa Praveen, Dilip Aher, and Nilesh Anute, Oxford University Press. © ASM Group of Institutes, Pune, India 2022. DOI: 10.1093/oso/9780192869418.003.0010

worked hard for securing sound and formidable partnerships, especially with the chipset manufacturers.

The Case

The history of Micromax (2011–2012 revenue: Rs 1,978 crore), which ventured into the mobile phone market in 2008, is one of the most fascinating success stories in the Indian consumer electronics industry. In barely five years, the company has come to occupy the third position (by volume) in the mobile handset market in India and is at No. 12 globally.

It leads the Indian tablet market with a share of 18.4%, ahead of veterans Samsung and Apple. The Gurgaon-headquartered company owes its success not just to the ticket it puts on its products or the speed with which it puts new designs on the shelves but to how it has managed these two crucial product inputs by leveraging China. To be more specific, the labour cost advantage and the production flexibility that China offered.

Big deal, you may say, given that almost every other handset brand in the world manufactures its products in China. Right from the Apple's to the Samsung's to many of our home-grown brands like Karbonn, a whole host of players reaped China's arbitrage advantage.

But here is the stumper: the strategy that offered Micromax its biggest advantage in its first five years is under threat and it will require a re-examination by the company and a number of other multinationals with Chinese production of their overall supply-chain strategies.

The reason is simple. At Shenzhen, where some of China's largest electronics manufacturers are located, the minimum wage is set for a 13.3% hike from this year a move that could have a ripple effect across the world's major technology companies.

According to some estimates, between 2005 and 2010, basic manufacturing wages in the country have soared roughly 70%. 'Eventually, Indian companies sourcing products and components from China need to develop local infrastructure. The reports of underage labourers and inhumane work conditions at some Chinese factories can have a cascading effect on the reputation of brands that source from China,' says a telecom expert.

What has made Micromax's life a little more complicated is its recent entry into categories like tablets and LED TVs. In short, if you were to add the increasing cost of monitoring suppliers and of compliance, that labour cost advantage Micromax enjoyed when it started out looks even more precarious.

To understand what Micromax needs to do here on, we need to first understand how the company harnessed China to reach the Top 5 bracket in the Indian mobile phone market. In an earlier interview, Rahul Sharma, co-founder, Micromax, had said:

'The strategy is simple: create high volumes, reach the customer base through effective distribution, give them products that are innovative and cost-effective. Finally, create a strong brand.' Micromax's strategy of associating with Bollywood and cricket has also helped. The company's advertising and marketing spend last year, according to experts, was to the tune of Rs 150 crore, which would be roughly what Britannia or Heinz spent on their brand communication that year.

What has also set Micromax apart is the speed at which it has been able to put products in the market and its tremendous reach. According to Mritunjay Kapur, country MD, Protiviti, the world's largest independent business and risk consulting firm, 'Players like Micromax are constantly pushing the product profile—they have been able to identify their markets well and be where the customer is.' So, where Micromax takes barely a month or two to launch products, another big international brand requires roughly 18 months for a similar product to go through the retail pipeline.

In effect, Micromax's growth strategy has followed three clear stages, explains an industry insider. When it started out, the company picked handsets from China, rebadged them and sold them in the India market. In the second stage, it realised the need to do extensive research in terms of Indian consumers' demands and product development. Now it has crossed over into a new phase, where the company has started following a mix-and-match strategy—getting some products manufactured in China and other countries, sourcing components from abroad and manufacturing some of the newer lines in India.

In a way, the changes in Micromax's growth strategy have followed the evolution of the mobile consumer in India. When it started its journey in 2008, the mobile phone market in India was pretty much a sellers' market.

'Consumers were adapting to what was being offered,' Micromax's Sharma says, 'We worked the other way round, trying to understand what the consumer's needs really were.' This focus on the consumer led to the launch of its first product—a phone with a 30-day power backup. 'People in Indian villages needed mobile handsets with enormous battery backup given the precarious electricity situation,' explained Sharma.

According to Anshul Gupta, principal research analyst, Gartner, a technology research firm, by getting products manufactured in China, Micromax could offer products at a price about 40% less than what other global players were offering. 'An Apple or a Samsung, which were also getting their products manufactured in China, would demand a mark-up based on the brand value; for a newcomer like Micromax that was never an issue. So they could offer similar features at a lower price,' says an industry hand.

'The basic strategy of Micromax has been "Affordable Innovation",' says an ex-employee of Micromax. In his view, the strategy at Micromax has always been clear: to look at four critical components of a phone which also determine its price. These include the screen, the camera, the chipset, and the memory used in the device. It's here that the cost of each model of handsets is determined. Deepak Mehrotra, chief executive officer at Micromax, says the company is driven by what customers want. So, the cost is also determined to what the consumer back home expects. 'So, if my target consumer doesn't particularly require a great camera feature, instead of giving a 8 megapixel camera, our handset will have a 5 megapixel one, which will obviously bring the price down,' explains Mehrotra.

'Pick up a box (of a mobile handset from any company) and you will see most are produced in China. The country clearly has built economies of scale and knows how to play it right. Why just us, manufacturing across categories is done in China, thanks to the cost efficiencies, eco-system and how they come together,' says Mehrotra.

Though Micromax didn't create 'reference designs' initially—preferring to simply give instructions to its third-party manufacturers in China—its winning strategy was to quickly start its R&D facility, create prototypes, and instruct contract manufacturers on what the company expected.

'The real clincher for Micromax was in identifying the Tier I rung of manufacturers, and then getting those manufacturers to work on our specifications, our innovations,' added the former Micromax employee. Right at the outset, Micromax took pains to mark out those manufacturers in China who were working with global brands. FoxConn, the world's largest contract manufacturer, for instance, has been associated with Apple products, according to the employee.

BYD, similarly, has been associated with Nokia production and also works on Micromax's handsets, he adds, saying that the company never bothered with the Tier II or the Tier III manufacturers where inferior quality of chipsets etc are used.

'For us, it was always the top tier of manufacturers—those who worked for the Apples and the Samsungs of the world that had to design our products too,' says this executive, adding that typically Micromax orders 5,00,000 handsets at the entry level from their contract manufacturers in China at one go. The volume growth in turn ensures better cost efficiencies. In 2011, for instance, Micromax shipped four million handsets worldwide in the second quarter. It cornered an 8% share in the home market, grew 48% annually and continues selling roughly 1.5 million phones every month in most of the countries that it operates in.

Besides leveraging the cost-effectiveness of China (Tier I manufacturers in China can typically charge $17 upwards per handset) says the ex-employee of Micromax, the company has worked hard at securing sound and formidable partnerships, especially with the chipset manufacturers.

On a New Wicket

Micromax's focus these days on is building its manufacturing infrastructure in India. 'It is a consumer durables company diversifying into other categories,' says Gupta of Gartner. Micromax's facility in Himachal Pradesh already manufactures television sets and some tablet models.

'Micromax now cannot afford to be just another "Fringe Player" that manufactures products in China and sells them in India,' says Kumar Kandaswami, senior director, Deloitte in India. 'Eventually, India needs to script a "China" story in terms of manufacturing its products at home,' he adds.

The reason is obvious: China is losing the advantage of labour cost arbitrage, a reason why even companies like Apple and GE have decided to shift product lines from China. 'Because Chinese wages are rising rapidly,' says an analyst, 'it makes sense to return manufacturing of a wide range of goods, with moderate levels of labour content and high logistics costs, to India.' Re-shoring may also make particular sense for bulky goods, like television sets, which naturally incur higher transportation costs.

'There are many hidden factors involved in sourcing heavy appliances from outside suppliers,' says a senior marketing executive with an appliances company. 'These variables include greater supply chain complexity, longer cycle times, quality issues and responsiveness to local demand. A local supply chain makes it easier for a company with a wide portfolio to respond to any sudden supply chain disruption or other unpredictable event.'

Not everyone thinks the China story is over though. Amitava Chattopadhyay, INSEAD Chair Professor in marketing and innovation, for example, says, 'China is a cheap manufacturing base for almost anything—toys, cars, electronics.' So, work will continue to happen in China.

But global players are setting up and growing their own facilities or scouting for opportunities in countries such as Vietnam, Indonesia and Cambodia to have greater control over cost and quality. 'Wherever you get economies of scale, it is good. It could be in China, Taiwan, or elsewhere,' says Mehrotra.

Ultimately, analysts believe that the correct balance can be struck through careful planning. And while Micromax grapples with supply chain issues, what works in its favour is that it is no longer a single product company and faces dilemmas that many other brands confront.

Conclusions

China is a cheap manufacturing base for almost anything—toys, cars, electronics—and hence handset's chip too. So Micromax focused on securing sound and formidable partnerships with the cheap manufacturing companies and launched rebadged handsets at an affordable price to Indian market. The Company also studied the requirement of Indian customer and released products accordingly.

That is the reason Micromax could able to create high volumes, and reach the customer base through effective distribution. Ultimately Apple and Samsung had to lag behind in the sales. The big volume order of 5,00,000 handsets is the evidence to this, and it so ensured the growth in turn over too. It is leveraged by the strategies adopted by them.

Case Questions

1. Do you think that the growth strategy (leveraging China) Micromax is sustainable in the long run?

2. How should Indian economist/strategists respond to such a cross country leveraging which is likely to drain business potential in the host country (India)?

3. In an economic situation being precarious more so in India with its political nuances how could one steer clear of possible business issues at both ends, i.e., China's rising labour costs and India's inability to fresh investments in industrial sectors?

11

Can 'HORLICKS' Be More Than a Health Drink?

Learning Objectives

Brands and products tend to age over the years if not nurtured properly. Horlicks has learnt to defy age. By successfully launching variants at different points in time, it has strengthened its core brand values, apart from addressing new consumer needs and thus bringing such consumers into its fold. Nevermore has success of a brand in India been so paradoxical than Horlicks from the GlaxoSmithKline Consumer Healthcare (GSKCH) stable. Conventional management wisdom will tell you to extract as much as you can from a brand and its variants but to derisk the owner from overdependence on the brand. But Horlicks is a case of repeated success with brand variants making a virtue of GSKCH's dependence on it. This case study looks at how Horlicks has avoided getting dated.

Synopsis

The case study discusses the transformation of Horlicks from a health drink meant for the elderly and the infirm to a nourishment drink for young children. It also describes the various strategies adopted by GlaxoSmithKline Beecham (GSK) such as introducing sub-brands and variations in the product range, improving the packaging, and advertising campaigns, etc., to change the image of the Horlicks brand. How the company diversified its target market in a bid to attract new consumers also forms a part of the case study.

Indian Business Case Studies. Roopa Praveen, Dilip Aher, and Nilesh Anute, Oxford University Press. © ASM Group of Institutes, Pune, India 2022. DOI: 10.1093/oso/9780192869418.003.0011

HORLICKS: A Household Name

Horlicks is a very powerful brand associated strongly with the milk and health space. This is both its strength and its weakness. GSKCH's health food drink (HFD) brands—Horlicks, Boost, Maltova, and Viva—account for 58.6% by value and 65.1% by volume of a Rs 5,000-crore market, as per market researcher Nielsen for 2013. Horlicks and its variants account for almost half the HFD market by volume. Cadbury India's Bournvita had a share of 17% and Heinz's Complan, 11%. Now, flip that inwards. The HFD category contributes 77% to GSKCH's revenues of Rs 3,079 crore for calendar 2012. So, really, how has the company fared in fortifying a brand that is 140 years old?

Horlicks was locally manufactured in India only since 1958, though it had been available via imports since the early 1900s. It was one of the early starters with aggressive advertising and it pulled in celebrities such as Amitabh Bachchan in the 1970s to endorse its brand over radio. But Horlicks remained largely a family drink till the 1990s.

The company then recognized that there was a specific need for toddlers in the one to three years age group and launched Junior Horlicks in 1995. It had made a bid for its first brand line-extension with biscuits in 1992, but that hardly moved the needle for the company. This was a period of turmoil in the consumer products market, as India, after liberalization, saw the entry of several new brands from both domestic and international players. Bournvita and Complan were seen to be strong contenders in west and northern parts of the country, so was local player Jagatjit Industries with its brand Maltova and Viva in the north. GSKCH acquired Maltova and Viva and effectively prevented competition from opening a new front.

It simultaneously invested in consumer research and aggressive brand strategy. 'We would visit homes and the company wanted to listen in to the consumer needs even in the early 1980s,' says Bindu Sethi, Chief Strategy Officer at ad agency JWT. She has been associated with the brand since then, first as part of market research firm IMRB and then when she joined HTA (now JWT) in 1988 as a media planner. 'It was this consumer voice that found reflection in the repositioning of Horlicks as a drink targeted at children in 2003, with the "Epang, Opang, Jhapang" campaign,' she says. This was the tipping point.

What appeared to be a natural slot for the brand to slip into actually followed heated debate within the company: Horlicks was a family drink until then, the great 'family nourisher'. All branding and communication spoke to different family members and how it meant different things to different people, while the new campaign spoke to children directly. 'There were worries that it would disengage a loyal adult base,' says Charubala Sheshadri, marketing director, Wellness (OTC) and Oral Health, GSKCH, who joined the company in 2004 as marketing manager for Horlicks.

Taller! Stronger! Sharper!

This campaign, however, was just the precursor. The company has always viewed Horlicks equity as a bank deposit since. 'It has invested at every critical juncture in the brand and its nutrition profile backing it with proof of science,' says Sheshadri.

In 2003, it offered its newly formulated Horlicks to the National Institute of Nutrition (NIN) at Hyderabad, which conducted research to prove its effect on the growth of children. 'We clearly identified three key benefit areas to do with bone health of children, muscle health and their ability to focus better,' says Singh. This led to the 'Taller, Stronger, Sharper' campaign. In this, the company tapped into the growing pester power of children who now were key decision-makers not only with what they ate, but also other key decisions around the household. There was someone else too, pushing for this change.

The company now had a new managing director in Zubair Ahmed in 2007. He inherited a company that had already accelerated into double-digit growth. By then, the company had speeded up its brand variant launches with Horlicks Lite in 2005, aimed at diabetics and Horlicks NutriBar in 2006 (this launch did not work as planned).

More Extensions

The company found that women were an ignored segment as there was no specific product addressing their specific need. This led to the launch of Women's Horlicks in 2008, creating a blockbuster product. 'It has been growing 60–65 per cent year on year [even if] on a small base,' says Singh. But the effect has been that Horlicks Lite combined with Women's Horlicks ensured that the company clocked growth of more than 17% in revenues until 2011. Given that competition was also pumping up volume on the benefit of micronutrients and research-backed offering, in 2012 GSKCH again decided to challenge itself to deliver further on its by-now older promise of 'Taller, Stronger, Sharper'. Aided by its R&D centre, it formulated a blend of Horlicks that was guided by its earlier study done by NIN. The results showed five clear areas of benefit: more bone area, more muscle, better concentration, more active nutrients, and healthier blood. This led to its launch of the '5 Signs of Growth' positioning and campaign.

Where It Failed?

GSKCH had its hiccups with its Horlicks extensions. The 2010 launch of Chill Dood, its flavoured milk range, did not take off. Nor did its attempt to launch cream biscuits and noodles, under the brand Horlicks Foodles, in 2009. 'I think it has huge potential in the health segment of biscuits with digestive, diabetic, milk, etc. However, in segments like noodles and snacking where taste is supreme, they will find it difficult to compete with the likes of Nestle and ITC,' says Alagh, the marketing consultant and former managing director of biscuit maker Britannia Industries.

According to Alagh, GSKCH needs to transform brand Horlicks from 'purely health, especially aimed at children, to a tasty but healthy positioning' for all. Therein lies the challenge. Industry insiders say much of the company's success has come from adjacent brand variants such as Horlicks Junior, Women's Horlicks, Horlicks Lite, and Mother's Horlicks and not from extensions into biscuits, noodles, and, even low-priced HFD variants such as Asha.

Latest extensions like Horlicks ProMind and Horlicks Gold are yet to establish themselves conclusively, though they have shown promising off-take in their test markets in the south. GSKCH thinks successes far outnumber failures. 'We are already the second-largest brand in the south after Quaker Oats,' points out Singh. GSKCH is certainly on a fast track.

According to the Ace Equity database, Horlicks and its brand variants have helped the company accelerate its revenues and profits in the last five years (till December 2012) to 19.2% and 23.4%, respectively, against 13.1 and 20.8% in the preceding five years. Taller, Stronger, Sharper, indeed.

Conclusions

What makes this case study a riveting read and apt for analysis is the paradox of creating a very strong brand. The students can compare this paradoxical situation of brand extension with reference to other strong brands like Colgate, Nirma, Pond's, and Lifebuoy as also weak brands like Vespa and Chik. Since the brand Horlicks has so far been successful only in launching variants to its malted beverage, the students can debate over the possibility of the brand developing an image of a healthy food option in some other related categories like porridge mix, protein shakes, convalescent diet products, or even dietary supplements like Ensure, etc.

Case Questions

1. What are the positioning strategies followed by GlaxoSmithKline Beecham for one of its successful brands 'Horlicks'?

2. How successful has Horlicks been in extending to new market segments through the launch of new variants appealing to all age groups?

Suggested Reading

http://www.gsk-ch.in/History.aspx
http://www.thehindubusinessline.com/features/investment-world/article1447
667.ece
https://m.economictimes.com/industry/cons-products/fmcg/horlicks-aims-rs-50-
crore-sales-from-biscuits/articleshow/4644931.cms
https://m.economictimes.com/news/company/corporate-trends/gsk-consumer-
will-pushing-horlicks-into-new-categories-destroy-the-brand/articleshow/7415
215.cms

12

Power of 10—'Full Throttle'

A VUCA Situation in Two-wheeler Segment

Learning Objectives

The business world has changed dramatically over the last few decades, and we are in a society where change is continuous and it is a fast-paced one. So it has become very essential to learn how to manage it as we cannot live without change. Changes are taking place due to technology, new methods adopted in work, changes in thought process of governments, crises across the globe due to environment or war fears. Global financial market slumps have also added fire to volatility and uncertainty. So in management it is said VUCA has to be dealt in a suitable manner.

Synopsis

The case deals with a specific sector in the VUCA (volatility, uncertainty, complexity, and ambiguity) market. The two-wheeler segment plays an important role in the Indian economy which was dominated by Bajaj for a very long period. After the domination of Bajaj two-wheelers came to an end various players have entered the market where almost a saturation point of the players emerged. So the case deals with this scenario of various players, uncertain as to what shall happen, every manufacturer wanting a foreign technically sound partner and no one knows how customer tastes can vary.

Indian Business Case Studies. Roopa Praveen, Dilip Aher, and Nilesh Anute, Oxford University Press. © ASM Group of Institutes, Pune, India 2022. DOI: 10.1093/oso/9780192869418.003.0012

The Case

Hero has forged an alliance with EBR for high-end bikes and sponsors the EBR team in America's premier motorcycle racing circuit. The 58-year-old big daddy of the world's largest two-wheeler company by volume is gearing up to go global at a time when doubting Thomas's point at dipping domestic sales, predicting an uncertain future for the two-wheeler company.

The CEO of a rival company says: 'Hero is in a place where Bajaj was many years ago—without a technology partner. The way things are moving in the motorcycles market, it's soon going to be a two-horse race between Honda and Bajaj. Honda on its own is a far more dangerous player than Hero Honda.'

In April–October 2012, Hero MotoCorp sold 3.4 million units and registered a negative growth of 1.83% over the same period the previous year. Bajaj Auto too shrank by 4.5% in the same period, while Honda Motorcycles and Scooters India (HMSI) grew by 47%, albeit on a much lower base of 1.5 million units. In the fast-growing scooter segment, Hero has a 17% market share, while Honda with 49.3% market share is by far the leader. The contest is rather close between Hero and TVS for the number two position.

What's going on? 'When Honda came out with a 100% subsidiary in India (HMSI in 1999), they manufactured only scooters for the first 5 years of their operation since that was the deal with us,' says Munjal, echoing how he fended off Honda's challenge in motorbikes long enough for Hero Honda to consolidate and add teeth to volumes.

But the hiatus proved a boon for Honda to develop a market for scooters at a time when the segment was sliding. For Hero, it will now indeed be difficult to unseat its established erstwhile partner in a rapidly growing segment.

Another significant shift can be noticed in the traction across the 125cc segment, a sort of aspirational up trading by customers. Traditionally, Hero has championed the 100cc segment and rules the roost with two-thirds of the market with winners, such as the Splendor and Passion. 'In a full year, Splendor sells about a third of our volumes,' claims Dua.

But over the years, Bajaj has built up capabilities in the 125cc space while Hero battles on with three offerings. 'Hero's relative advantage will get whittled away as the competition already has credible products in the 125cc space,' says a recent report from CitiGroup.

Even in the premium segment, Hero's heroics come unstuck. Its market share was down to 7% in August from 24% five quarters ago. Blame it on the slowdown for now, but as the segment continues to grow, Hero may have to bite the bullet from Bajaj (40% market share) and Honda (17%).

Nevertheless, it's worth noting that with approximately 70% share in the most popular 100cc segment of the two-wheeler industry, Hero has penetrated deep into the hinterland with almost 5,400 touch points encompassing dealerships, service, and spare parts outlets and authorized reps of dealers, while nearest competitor Bajaj stands a distant second with 3,500 touch points. 'We will be adding another 400 touch points to our network by the end of this year (taking the total to 5800),' says Anil Dua, senior vice president-sales and marketing, Hero MotoCorp, when grilled on the Honda challenge.

With the success of the Hero Honda venture behind him, Dua revs up for a repeat performance. 'I'm not very concerned about market shares going up and down,' he says matter-of-factly, pointing to a newfound vigour post the split with Honda. 'I'm looking ahead.' In a volume-driven market like India where competition is hotting up, despite being market leaders, Hero has stepped up its efforts to go overseas. 'We've created an international business division with 16 people as of now and want to grow our international business five times in five years,' says Dua. Earlier, Hero Honda had just two people in its overseas division and exported to four countries-Nepal, Sri Lanka, Bangladesh, and Colombia—accounting for a mere 3% of its annual turnover. Today, the thinking has changed even though the turning of the tide can take longer.

1. Adding 400 touch points by yearend taking dealership network to 5,800 in FY2012–13.
2. Setting up an international business division to scout for global markets and overseas manufacturing potential.
3. Forging alliances with three separate global players in the automotive space—Erik Buell Racing (EBR) of the US for high-end bikes, Austria-based AVL for engine technologies, and Italian design firm Engines Engineering (EE) for end-to-end two-wheeler design solutions.

4. Planned Rs 400 crore investments to set up a fully integrated R&D centre at Kukas, Rajasthan. Built over an area of 250 acre, the centre will be the largest two-wheeler R&D set up in the country, which will have over 500 engineers.

5. The company targets US$10 billion in turnover in five years with 10 million unit volumes and 10% of total volumes to come from international business

While unveiling the new brand identity in London O2 Arena last year, Munjal outlined the vision of his company through the Power of 10. Simply put, in five years, he's eyeing $10 billion in revenues with 10 million units, and at least 10% of the total volumes coming from the international business. Very carefully, the company has recalibrated the nomenclature from 'exports' to 'international business', since it harbours hopes of setting up manufacturing facilities in some of the newer geographies it is venturing into.

'We've appointed distributors in Africa, Central America and Latin America and are first tapping those markets where we believe our products will deliver', claims Munjal in the backdrop of Bajaj Auto's successful foray in the overseas markets, which now forms one-third of its total business by volume.

Changing Scenario

Along with Erik Buell Racing of the USA, Hero has also tied up with AVL of Austria for engine technologies and Italian design firm Engines Engineering (EE) for end-to-end two-wheeler design solutions—who are working together to develop the next-generation Hero two-wheelers. Hero is reportedly working on several models ranging from low engine displacement to higher-powered motorcycles and scooters. However, the first bike on a new platform to hit the market will be a 250cc motorcycle by the third or fourth quarter of FY2014–15.

Ever since Hero separated from Honda, the company has launched only four products, which could all be termed as Honda's babies in terms of technology. The Honda effect may well continue with a couple of fresh launches in the next fiscal. But does that augur well for the group when the competition has the firepower to deliver more? 'In the first 15 years of this company (1985–2000), we launched only six models. From 2001 to 2005, the company launched 15 models. Each year now, companies launch on an average 8–10 models,' says Ravi Sud, Senior VP & CFO, Hero MotoCorp. Clearly, Hero falls woefully short of market expectations in the near term.

But the new tie-ups will surely come into force after that and Munjal is upbeat. 'The premium segment is currently on the drawing board, well beyond the design board, and we've seen mock-ups and clay models ... in 2014, we would have a completely new portfolio.'

It is learnt that the first bike from Hero will sport a 250cc engine. But sceptics differ, as analysts question the effectiveness of the tie-ups, save AVL, a trusted name in engine technologies.

'While EBR is a boutique, EE is not a name to reckon with in auto design,' says an analyst requesting anonymity. There is also hint of an apprehension of a complete tech overhaul from the existing Japanese platform to the western domain.

Dua dispels that fear. 'Instead of completely replacing what our erstwhile partner has done, we need to know about engines, we need inputs on designing and styling, we need to know about racing,' he says adding that currently, Hero engineers are working with these partners to 'co-develop' the company's future SKU's.

Clearly, the competitors and market watchers know Hero still has a strong franchise and the massive transformation exercise will build a strong platform. 'Hero has seen 70 years of evolution under Brij Mohan Munjal. Their understanding of the market is very deep.

The competition can have better technology but that's not sufficient to win the market. Therefore, dislodging the current lead of Hero will be difficult for the competitors,' says Ramdeo Agarwal, Jt. MD of Motilal Oswal. 'In this very sector, there have been past instances of promoters doing well, in spite of their JV partners walking out. So there is no reason why Hero can't repeat that,' adds Ravi Sardana, EVP, and ICICI Securities.

Market watchers say Munjal's chemistry with stakeholders may not be as strong as his father's, Chairman Brij Mohan Munjal, around whom legends of benevolence have been woven. A source even said that once when an employee needed blood, it was Sr. Munjal who came to his rescue by donating his own blood. And the same thread of deep relationships runs through the dealers and distributors as well. Just when CD was interviewing Hero executives Brij Mohan Munjal and his wife passed through the reception of the Hero MotoCorp HQ. A couple of dealers standing at the reception offered him belated Diwali gifts and touched his feet. He blessed them and asked how they were doing, whether they faced any hiccups-all in first name terms.

Conclusions

However, the larger question is whether Hero will remain a two-wheeler company. 'It's about mobility and if Hero Moto Corp is a two wheeler company today, it could be anything tomorrow,' says Dua—hinting at larger plays in auto. And he believes that unity of command allows room for such adventures. 'It enables you to do visioning, missioning, give a strategic thrust, alignment and then a plan to go for it and execute that plan,' he says. With a heatwave as severe as one is witnessing in the two-wheeler category, Hero has a tough battle at hand. The overseas thrust may be one way to battle the crisis but a category leap calls for another round of introspection.

Case Questions

1. What in your opinion are the possibilities of Hero group maintaining its leadership status with the exit of Honda from its stable?

2. Do you think the Power of Ten strategy is feasible? If yes how?

13

An Audacious Acquisition

A Case Study on Major Global Acquisition

Learning Objectives

Mergers and acquisitions are major strategies for the inorganic growth of any organization. If it happens to be severely fought attempt to acquire a company in spite of its promoters opposition it becomes more interesting to learn as to how such acquisitions need to be tactfully managed.

Mittal Steels strong desire to acquire the assets of the global leader in Auto steel Arcelor basically with an intention to grow the market size and scope of technology of manufacture is an example of how a strong business sense and focused line of action disarms all attempts to sabotage the acquisition.

This case study will help the companies wanting to look for global opportunities for inorganic growth as also the students and faculty in the learning and teaching process in strategic management of business growth.

Synopsis

In the year 2009 entire world of business has witnessed one of the most hostile and terribly audacious but finally fruitful take over the move by M/S Mittal Steel NV of M/S Arcelor NV of Luxemburg. It was really an equivalent of the 'World Cup' event for the Mergers and acquisitions activity ever seen under the normal business circumstances.

Indian Business Case Studies. Roopa Praveen, Dilip Aher, and Nilesh Anute, Oxford University Press. © ASM Group of Institutes, Pune, India 2022. DOI: 10.1093/oso/9780192869418.003.0013

As much as it has been a 'Battle of the Nerves' for both the parties, it was also an item of international 'Pride and Prejudice' for the countries to which the individual businesses belonged. The world government was also interested in the outcome of this bout.

Perhaps M/S Arcelor NV the World's No.1 Steel Manufacturer was not very much aware of its vulnerability of the take-over attempts and perhaps less aware of an Indian business man making such an attack from the front.

The friendly presumably covert moves made by Mr Aditya Mittal (the CFO of Mittal Steel) of getting closer to few of the senior executives of Arcelor perhaps did not indicate the potential time bomb of acquisition which he was carrying in his armoury during his meetings with Arcelor.

Mr Aditya (Adit to his family) Mittal has now surfaced to be one of the youngest business tycoons capable of baring the deadliest typhoons on the shores of the international business.

While being reasonably ambitious Mr Aditya Mittal, who now as per the international media has turned out to be the kingpin of the takeover bid, has been extremely shrewd, confident and shown his ability to muster not only the approval of his proposal by the top-level management committee at Mittal's but also could make his father Mr Laxmi Nivas Mittal take up the issue like a Shark insight of a prey, never stops till the result is achieved.

The media in its all fronts was also getting in a dilemma as to the status and the final outcome of the acquisition war. One magazine of National Repute printed on its cover 'WHAT WENT WRONG?' as a cover story while writing about Mittal's acquisition for the edition dated 18 July 2006 and within 48 hours the entire situation literally turned around and Mr L. N. Mittal made a public statement on 24 June that the merger talks were nearing a favourable conclusion for his company. This happened in spite of quite a few global giants concluding that the deal has failed and has become a part of history.

The Case Details

It was a warm sunny day in Brussels. It was just past noon. Lakshmi Niwas Mittal the world's largest steel maker was meeting Joseph Kinsch, chairman of Arcelor. Mittal had made the most audacious bid for the second-largest steel company. After three long hours they broke up. The deal seemed to be in favour of Mittal's. That was 18 June 2006.

The Mittals of M/S LN Mittal Steel

Lakshmi Niwas Mittal has a reputation built on his ability to take over companies, turn them around, and make profits. Mittal Steel is the world's largest and a global steel producer. It is the largest steel producer in the Americas and Africa and the second largest in Europe. Mittal Steel is a successor to a business founded in 1989 by Mr Lakshmi.

N. Mittal, the Chairman and Chief Executive Officer. Mittal Steel has experienced a rapid and steady growth since then, largely through the consistent and disciplined execution of a successful consolidation strategy. A strategy that has taken him from a 23 million tpa steelmaker to the world's largest.

Arcelor Steels Luxemburg

While on the other hand Arcelor was created in February 2002 by three steel-making companies, Aceralia Corporatión Siderurgica, Arbed, and Usinor. Arcelor is the second-largest steel producer in the world in terms of production. Arcelor is the market leader in Western Europe; 71.2% of its sales in 2005 were in the European Union. Arcelor also has a strong position in South America, particularly due to its Brazilian operations.

Arcelor has made several significant acquisitions, particularly in South America and Eastern Europe. Most recently, Arcelor acquired Dofasco, a leading Canadian steelmaker, for C$5.6 billion. Arcelor used subtle and not so subtle tactics to attack Mittal's ethnicity but Mittal got the Indian government to bat for him.

It was one of the toughest challenges for Mittal so far. Although the business logic and the business plan made some sense for the share-holders, there was a stronger base required on the grounds of Corporate Governance and value proposition. It was a merger to take place among equals.

In June 2001, Mittal Steel adopted corporate governance guidelines that is considered to be in line with best practices of corporate governance. Mittal Steel monitored new, proposed, and final U.S. and Dutch corporate regulatory requirements and made adjustments to its corporate governance controls and procedures to stay in compliance with these requirements on a timely basis. Mittal Steel was committed to meeting the corporate governance mandates and requirements under applicable current and proposed Dutch Civil Code.

Mr L.N. Mittal launched the formal offer in May. Arcelor wasn't giving in easily and ridiculed the offer to an ordinary 'cologne' compared to the 'perfume that Arcelor was'.

Arcelor CEO Mr Dolle brought in a 'white knight' in the form of Alexei Mordashov, a billionaire who ran the Russian Severstal. On 26 May Arcelor announced a deal with Severstal that would give it a controlling stake in Russia's largest steelmaker and stall the audacious overtures for Mr L.N. Mittal.

Mr Dolle has gone on record to call Mr Mittal's proposal to lure Arcelor shareholders as 'Monkey Money', perhaps this was the beginning of the loss of share-holder confidence in Arcelor. Mr Dolle even undermined the prerequisite of minimum 50% of Arcelor shareholders to approve its acquisition of M/S Severstal of Russia. This was the 'Waterloo' for Arcelors adamant stance of not allowing Mittals to even communicate with them.

Overview of the Case

About the Mittals

Mittal Steel is a successor to a business founded in 1989 by Mr Lakshmi N. Mittal, its chairman and Chief Executive Officer.

Mittal Steel has experienced rapid and steady growth since then, largely through the consistent and disciplined execution of a successful consolidation-based strategy of acquisitions of sick large scale steel plants and turning them around to profit.

Mittal Steel Company N.V. is a Dutch public limited liability company incorporated on 27 May 1997.

By 31 March 2006, the controlling of the economic rights of the shareholders was 98.32% of the combined voting by the Mittal's in Mittal Steel NV.

Mittal Steel is the world's largest and a global steel producer. It is the largest steel producer in the Americas and Africa and the second largest in Europe. Mittal Steel produces a broad range of high-quality finished and semi-finished steel products, structural sections, and rails.

Mittal Steels have a high degree of geographic diversification. Mittal Steel has access to high-quality and low-cost raw materials through its captive sources and long-term contracts. Mittal Steel is one of the world's largest producers of coke.

Mittal Steel has research and development (R&D) expertise in both product development and manufacturing processes.

Under Mittal Steel's Articles of Association and the Management Board Rules and Dutch corporate law, the members of the Board of Directors are collectively responsible for the management, general and financial affairs, and policy and strategy of Mittal Steel and its group companies.

The executive directors are responsible for managing the day-to-day business and operations of Mittal Steel as well as other responsibilities that have been delegated to the executive directors in accordance with Dutch law and Mittal Steel's Articles of Association.

The Board of Directors has an Audit Committee, a Nomination Committee, and a Remuneration Committee, each of which is comprised solely of the independent (non-executive) directors, with written charters that are published on Mittal Steel's website.

Summary of the Offer

Mittal Steel offered to acquire Arcelor shares and Convertible Bonds through two separate offers:

a. The European Offer
b. The U.S. Offer.

(The settlement of the European Offer and the U.S. Offer was to be effected concurrently.)

The European Offer is in principle governed by the takeover regulations of the jurisdictions where the European Offer is made to the public.

The U.S. Offer will be made in compliance with applicable U.S. tender offer procedural rules, which have been reflected in the terms and conditions of the Offer as described by the company.

Corporate Governance Issues

In June 2001, Mittal Steel adopted corporate governance guidelines that is considered to be in line with best practices of corporate governance.

Mittal Steel monitors new, proposed and final U.S. and Dutch corporate regulatory requirements and makes adjustments to its corporate governance controls and procedures to stay in compliance with these requirements on a timely basis.

Mittal Steel is committed to meeting the corporate governance mandates and requirements under applicable current and proposed SEC regulations and NYSE listing standards and the laws of The Netherlands.

During the Mittal Steel annual general meeting of shareholders held on 26 May 2005, Shareholders approved amendments to Mittal Steel's Articles of Association to reflect recent changes in Dutch company law as contained in Book 2 of the Dutch Civil Code.

Arcelor NV

Arcelor was created in February 2002 by three steel-making companies, Aceralia Corporación Siderurgica, Arbed, and Usinor.

The Arcelor group operates in four market sectors: Flat Carbon Steels, Long Carbon Steels, Stainless Steels, and Arcelor Steel Solutions and Services. Arcelor is the second-largest steel producer in the world in terms of pro-duction.

Arcelor is the market leader in Western Europe; 71.2% of its sales in 2005 were in the European Union. Arcelor also has a strong position in South America, particularly due to its Brazilian operations.

Arcelor has made several significant acquisitions, particularly in South America and Eastern Europe. Most recently, Arcelor acquired

Dofasco, a leading Canadian steelmaker, for C$5.6 billion. Arcelor S.A. is a Luxembourg public limited liability company.

Risk Factors

For Mittals

Mittal Steel has not been given the opportunity to conduct a due diligence review of the non-public records of Arcelor. Therefore, Mittal Steel may be subject to unknown liabilities of Arcelor that may have a material adverse effect on Mittal Steel's profitability and results of operations.

The existence of minority interests in Arcelor's share capital may reduce the anticipated benefits of the Offer to Mittal Steel.

Mittal Steel is a Dutch company, and being a shareholder of a Dutch company involves different rights and privileges than being a shareholder of a Luxembourg company.

Mittal Steel must make a mandatory tender offer for minority interests in Arcelor's listed Brazilian subsidiaries at a price determined by independent experts, which may be higher than expected.

Mittal Steel will substantially increase its outstanding debt in connection with the acquisition of Arcelor, which may lower its credit rating. Cyclical downturns in the steel industry could also lead to credit rating downgrades. Credit rating downgrades could significantly harm Mittal Steel's refinancing capacity, increase its cost of funding, and limit its flexibility in managing its business.

Mittal Steel has not verified the reliability of the Arcelor information included in this Information Document.

Investors may sell Mittal Steel shares that they receive in the Offer, which could put pressure on the market price of the Mittal Steel shares following the Offer.

For Arcelor

The consummation of the offer could trigger the change of control payments in the employment agreements of certain members of Arcelor's senior management, as well as change of control provisions in other contracts of Arcelor.

In certain limited circumstances, Mittal Steel has the right to withdraw and terminate the Offer at any time until the settlement date of the Offer, including during the period between the end of the acceptance period and the settlement date. In this case, the value of Arcelor Securities may decrease during the period between their tender in the Offer and the return of such securities.

It is possible that the acceptance period for the European Offer may be extended beyond the 30th Business Day following its commencement, which would prolong uncertainty as to the ultimate outcome of the Offer and would delay an Arcelor security holder's ability to receive consideration for tendered securities.

If the Offer is successful, the liquidity and market value of Arcelor Securities not tendered in the Offer may be significantly reduced.

For Both

The consideration offered for Arcelor shares may be adjusted at any time prior to settlement in the event of certain actions taken in relation to Arcelor's net equity.

The fixed exchange ratio will not reflect market fluctuations.

Even if Mittal Steel consummates the Offer, there may be a delay before Mittal Steel can obtain management control of Arcelor.

Regulatory approvals of the Offer may not be obtained or may impose adverse conditions and obligations.

The integration of the operations of Arcelor and Mittal Steel may not be fully successful and the integration process may disrupt operations.

Consummation of the Offer may negatively impact Mittal Steel's or Arcelor's corporate tax position.

Mr Lakshmi N. Mittal can appoint Mittal Steel's directors and determine the outcome of shareholder votes. If the Offer is completed, other holders will be unable to determine the outcome of shareholder votes with respect to most corporate events.

Intentions of the Acquisition (As Explained to the Media and Public by the Mittals)

Rationale of the Offer

Mittal Steel believes 'the need to expand quickly into emerging markets where future growth will be highest, the drive for greater economies of scale in plant utilization and research and development ("R&D"), and the overall objectives of reducing earnings volatility and creating sustainable returns on capital. (Arcelor's senior management has similarly noted the need and desirability of industry rationalization and consolidation.)'

Mittal Steel considers that the combination of Mittal Steel and Arcelor (together, the 'Group') has a strong strategic and economic rationale. It represents a step-change in consolidation, which will bring together two largely complementary businesses in terms of both geographic presence and product offerings, to create a European based, leading global steel supplier with approximately 10% of worldwide crude steel production.

Mittal Steel believes that the combination will lead to better service to a globalizing customer base, more effective purchasing from concentrated suppliers, lower production costs, enhanced R&D, better resistance to volatility in what traditionally has been a highly cyclical industry, and improved access to growth opportunities in emerging economies.

It expects the combination to generate cost synergies in the range of US$1.0 billion (830 million) annually by 2009 (approximately 1.5% of the Group's sales in 2005) from a combination of purchasing savings and improved logistics (US$600 million), manufacturing and process optimization (US$200 million), and marketing and trading (US$200 million). As evidenced by numerous statements by both Mittal Steel and Arcelor, both companies see industry consolidation as an important strategic objective.

The proposed combination would turn both companies' vision into reality for the benefit of all stakeholders. Mittal Steel believes that the large global producers will have a number of common characteristics:

Mittal Steel believes also that growth rates combined with consolidation trends will move the leadership threshold closer to 150–200 million tonnes by 2015. This target represents 12 to 15% of the global steel market expected by 2015.

Strong business relationships with increasingly global customers make global key account management, including services through state-of-the-art downstream operations, distribution, and global product capabilities, even more crucial. Multi-regional operations to capitalize on R&D and process innovations.

Integration into mining operations and integrating upstream will reduce raw material price volatility (hedging). This has been one of the key elements of Mittal Steel's strategy over the last 15 years.

World-class sustainable development practices and operational excellence. Knowledge sharing and technology transfer will improve operational performance. Mittal Steel's success has stemmed from its ability to share experiences and best practices across the whole group between units spread around the world. Continuous improvement is a key driver within Mittal Steel.

Mittal Steel believes that large transactions, such as the combination with Arcelor, can create a global leadership position faster, more efficiently and with less risk than a series of medium-sized acquisitions and organic growth.

Mittal Steel and Arcelor Are
Highly Complementary

Arcelor and Mittal Steel have been following a similar strategy in recent years with respect to growth by acquisitions, particularly in emerging markets. Mittal Steel has been a pioneer, acquiring over 20 companies of various sizes and activities, and in a variety of world regions, over the last 15 years.

Mittal Steel and Arcelor are committed to substantial levels of capital investment.

Mittal Steel practices disciplined capital management. This investment represents a commitment to maintaining its existing asset base at a competitive level of productivity and quality while growing capabilities in important geographic and market segments.

Arcelors capital expenditures amounted to €1.4 billion in 2004 and €2.1 billion in 2005. The complementary footprint and product offering of Mittal Steel and Arcelor will give the Group a clear leadership position in the automotive industry.

The combined group will be an industry leader better able to serve US and European auto manufacturers, the respective businesses of Mittal Steel and Arcelor show a high degree of complementarily in that they are focused on similar customers and similar products but in different geographical markets.

Both Mittal Steel and Arcelor have similar overall growth plans for developing markets but have started in different locations, and both companies favour greater vertical integration but Mittal Steel is more developed upstream while Arcelor is more developed downstream.

Along the value chain, the two companies have complementary positions. Mittal Steel is more vertically integrated upstream, providing access to raw materials supply, while Arcelor is more integrated downstream.

- R&D and product offerings are complementary.
- Both Arcelor and Mittal Steel have the capabilities to produce innovative high-end products in partnership with customers.
- R&D synergy between Mittal Steel and Arcelor.

The expertise of both groups in the various applications and end markets, along with the large R&D divisions of the Group in Europe and North America, can be combined to generate new leverage and market opportunities from the cross-sharing of experience.

Mittal Steel believes that its position in raw materials would be an asset for the Group, enabling it to better absorb cyclical fluctuations in demand and to reduce volatility. Economic performance varies along the value chain.

Arcelor would benefit from Mittal Steel's access to raw materials self-sufficient steelmakers. Arcelor's strong position in downstream distribution would create benefits for both groups. The geographical range of the two groups is highly complementary.

The combined entity will be a global leader with a capacity of approximately 130 million tonnes, the Group will have a production 2.9 times that of its nearest competitor, which comparatively provides the Mittal Steel-Arcelor combination with financial strength and ample resources.

View from the Top

Mittal Steel believes that the combination will create a global industry leader, with unprecedented scale and growth opportunities and the opportunity to increase its technological advantage by strengthening its R&D to better focus on its customers' needs. Mittal Steel-Arcelor will be a leader in the automotive and domestic appliances industries. The Group will be able to bolster this strong product offering by deepening business relationships with its customers through a state-of-the-art global distribution network.

On the cost side, the global presence will allow further optimization of industrial operations. Mittal Steel believes that its access to low-cost production sites, as well as to mining assets, will afford some protection against fluctuations in raw material costs. In addition, the Group can realize significant synergies without major disruptions.

Implications of the Strategy for Arcelor
(As Seen by Mittal Steel)

Employment Opportunities

Mittal Steel anticipates no negative impact on the overall level of employment in Western Europe as a result of the combination.

Further, Mittal Steel believes that the overall growth of the Group will likely lead to increased employment in managerial positions in Europe, as has occurred following prior acquisitions in Central and Eastern Europe in the marked expansion of its Rotterdam corporate office.

Mittal Steel intends to provide for employee representation on the Board of Directors of the Group, and the practice of European works council will be maintained.

The role of R&D will be enhanced. Greater capital efficiency, with savings to be re-invested in other value-creation activities.

Mittal Steel's external growth policy will be to continue to make targeted investments and acquisitions, particularly in the higher growth BRICET countries.

The Synergies

Mittal Steel expects to realize synergies at least of US$1 billion (approximately 830 million) before taxes within three years of the combination. These synergies are in addition to the savings that are expected under the companies' respective existing plans to reduce costs. Purchasing savings should amount to US$600 million per year by 2009.

Marketing and trading synergies should generate US$200 million per year within three years. The estimated savings of US$200 million (€165 million) from manufacturing and process optimization are expected to result from manufacturing process improvements and yield gains, which will provide savings on raw materials and energy consumption, and productivity gains relating to higher throughput rates and better sequencing rates, which will improve asset utilization. On a production of approximately 100 million tonnes, this implies a cost savings of US$2 per tonne on a US$400/tonne cost base.

Mittal Steel expects to realize on an annualized basis approximately US$600 million in synergies by the end of the first year following the acquisition; the costs of implementing these synergies are estimated to be insignificant, since they require no restructuring or redundancies.

Finally, in the medium term, Mittal Steel expects further benefits, which have not yet been quantified, to accrue through ongoing knowledge sharing.

Corporate Governance (As per the Mittal Steel)

Mittal Steel's vision is to build the world's most admired steel institution. Mittal Steel's corporate culture is based on a spirit of entrepreneurship, diversity, and, most importantly, respect for employees, and seeks to promote the qualities of openness, expertise, reliability, and innovation.

Mittal Steel has a non-hierarchical structure, especially designed to encourage managers at all levels to think entrepreneurially, to make decisions in the best interests of the company, to take responsibility, and to support one another in all efforts to continually improve the company. Mittal Steel believes that Arcelor shares these values and that the strength of the Group will arise from the culture and principles that will unify all employees.

Management Mittal Steel will allocate management responsibilities on the basis of the best available talent within Mittal Steel and Arcelor, and the current expectation is that a substantial number of management positions in the Group will be allocated to current members of Arcelor's management. Mittal Steel will continue to employ best practices across the organization designed to meet the highest standards in health and safety, social responsibility, cultural diversity, and respect for the environment.

The acquisition of Arcelor substantially enlarges and deepens the talent pool and new and innovative ways of conducting business. The group will have a sustainable future and therefore sustainable employment in the competitive steel market.

Creating Uncertainty—To Put Pressure on Arcelor to the Agreement

The audacity, fierce fullness, commitment, and overall maturity shown by Mittal Steel in turning over a concluded failure into resounding, nail-biting 'success'.

Mr L N Mittal, chief architect of the takeover move and ably supported by his son Aditya Mittal and scores of senior executives and advisors to Mittals have exhibited extreme commitment, aggressiveness and timely maturity in the entire episode. Few to name (which got media attention) are as follows:

Mr L N Mittal swiftly moved to New Delhi in the guise of attending his friend's daughter's wedding to bring about a meeting between India's Prime Minister Dr Manmohan Singh (whom Mr Mittal had briefed beforehand the entire socio-political environment in the deal) and the French President Mr Jac Chirac). Dr Manmohan Singh tried to persuade

Mr Chirac to review Mittal's case of Arcelor's takeover bid. This definitely was an excellent move to strengthen the roots for a possible takeover.

Mr Kamal Nath, Cabinet minister for Industries and Commerce, was motivated to make a statement during the WTO meet (happened in Doha around the same time) that 'Globalization should be viewed as a two way affair and not the luxury of developed countries alone', hinting thereby the nascent opposition and restlessness among the leaders of the G8 companies to Mittal's proposed take over.

Mr Guy Dolle, MD of Arcelor SA made atrocious, instigating statements to undermine and blemish the capability of Mittals and calling them as 'Ordinary Cologne' compared to Arcelor who according to him was fragrant 'French Perfume'. He also called Mittal's offer as 'Monkey Money'. Mr L.N Mittal and his crack team members exhibited utmost patience and high level of maturity in not reacting to the instigative calls of the CEO of Arcelor.

Mr L N Mittal has shown grace by confirming Mr Kinshe as the chairman of Arcelor Mittal NV. Besides having employee representation on the board. He has exhibited extreme shrewdness by playing his cards extremely diligently and carefully.

Mr L N Mittal when asked by the media as what he feels about Mr Guy Dolle who was the real villain in the game, he was prompt to respond that he has high regards for Mr Dolle and he will look forward to Mr Dolle's guidance in the Arcelor Mittal venture. Mr Aditya Mittal declined to join the board of Arcelor Mittal by publically stating that he 'needs still more training and experience in managing things at Mittal's'. This again was a gracious move by the young Mittal in respecting the 'seniors' in the deal.

Mr Mittal did not lose time to profusely thank and convey his happiness to all Governments (starting with India) and well-wishers who supported him during his trying times in the entire episode of bitter battle during the takeover.

A Miraculous Merger: Birth of a Behemoth

Ultimately Howsoever Audacious the Mittals were, Mittal Steel Succeeded in their bid to acquire stakes in Arcelor. This changed Arcelor's DNA to Arcelor Mittal Steel w. e. f. 25 June 2006.

Case Questions

1. What really clinched the issue 'Mittal's Strategy' or Arcelor's lack of self-belief?

2. What was the real turning point of this hostile romance between Arcelor and Mittals?

3. Will this merger lead to confidence amongst the other businesses (specifically Indian origin) to make bolder moves towards consolidation to global acquisitions? Various national governments would take appropriate precautionary steps and formulate deterrent regulations to prevent such hostile takeovers and loss of national pride?

4. Will it make businesses feel insecure and nervous in the capability to manage their businesses without the fear of a takeover?

14

A Colourful 'Canvas'—Avc Ltd

A Case Study on the Mad Rush for Introduction of Newer Models and Technology in the TV Market in Early 2000s

Learning Objectives

The consumer durables market has always been a busy 'bee hive' like situation especially when the Television Technology invaded the otherwise cooler situations in Films and Casset players, etc.

The flood of TV sets with eye-catching colours and shapes and ever-changing technology adopting state of art chip technology replacing the electronic valves from global manufacturers disrupting the plans of all domestic manufacturers of Cassette Recorders and players who at times felt a suicidal situation they are confronted with so suddenly.

This case study takes the readers through the situations the existing manufacturers went through and how soon they could take up strategic change management and continued to survive and sustain.

Case Details

In the boardroom were Mohanlal Nair, president and Chief Operating Officer; Hari Zagade, general manager, Works; Ananya D'Souza, general manager, Marketing, Sundaram Iyer, general manager, Human Resources; and Rajiv Thakker, general manager, Finance. The preliminary greetings over, Advaith immediately got to the crux of the matter. 'I am sure that all of you are aware of the current market scenario. Our position as the leader in the color television (CTVs) segment is under threat. On the one hand, strong and sustained competition from the MNCs

Indian Business Case Studies. Roopa Praveen, Dilip Aher, and Nilesh Anute, Oxford University Press. © ASM Group of Institutes, Pune, India 2022. DOI: 10.1093/oso/9780192869418.003.0014

especially at the higher end is squeezing our margins. On the other hand, domestic players by producing cheaper CTVs are slowly eroding our market share.'

At this point Mohanlal interrupted, 'But the picture is not so bleak! We have a strong brand image, one of the best distribution networks in the country and large scale manufacturing capacity,' 'I agree,' continued Advaith, 'I also agree before you mention it, that there is immense potential in the yet untapped semi-urban and the rural market.

But to sustain our leadership position we will have to make huge dent in these markets and sustain current market share. Moreover, there is no denying the fact that we are not doing as well as earlier. Production may be up from 2.9bn units in 2000 to 4.7bn in FY2006, and sales have no doubt doubled from Rs6bn in FY01 to Rs. 17bn in FY86, but our market share figures are disturbing. Over the past three years, we have skidded from a high of 30% in FY84 to the current 26%. I don't think this is a blip, it is a trend.'

Financial Fumbles

'I agree, Sir,' butted in Rajiv. 'I took the liberty of preparing some data for us to mull over.' While the overhead projector was being set up, Rajiv circulated ACV's key financial parameters to the entire Leadership Team. 'The key point I would like to stress at the juncture is our high inventory cost and the level of our outstanding which is affecting the organization's profitability. We need to think of ways to improve working capital. I've based interest costs at the usual 12%.'

Hari threw a sidelong glance at his colleague, wondering whether to set the record straight or not, then decided to plunge in. 'As you know, we have an installed capacity of 1.3mn CTv's and home theatre sets at our there production facilities at Cochin, Noida and Bangalore,' he began. 'The color picture tube a CTVs major component is procured from three suppliers who are located at Ghaziabad, Secunderabad and Mumbai. This has resulted in an increase in transportation and distribution costs. We buy picture tubes of size 14", 20721" and 25729" from these supplies and all of them have adequate production capacity of all the three sizes.

Roughly 30% the total raw material and stores cost is from imported components.'

'The corner stone of AVCs marketing strategy is quality,' continued Hari. 'Traditionally we have prided ourselves on being one of the best television manufactures in India.'

The successful launch of the brands Web TV and Designer TV has created waves and ripples in the market. I don't need to tell this group that one of the key factors contributing to AVC's reputation for quality has been our effort to avoid price competition and instead concentrate on building the best product technically possible.

Hari was prepared to argue with Rajiv but an attack from a different flank left him winded. 'That's true,' pointed out Sundaram, 'but you will also have to admit that over a period of time, the systems and procedures of the company have become static and this has resulted in a lot of rigidity in the shop floor. This has also given rise to inter and intra- departmental conflicts. The union has become strong in terms of their demands and is not prepared to have flexibility in operations. An offshoot of this is the increase in inventory cost, obsolescence and thefts.' 'I have discussed the situation with the production planning and control manager, stores manager and purchase manager,' continued Sundaram.

'The meeting revealed that there was no proper application of supply chain decided to use logistic systems for better management of inbound and outbound services and also implement inventory control techniques.'

'The company has a strong union and it is now becoming a hindrance to productivity,' a visibly upset Hari pointed out. 'We have lost nearly twenty man-days during the last financial years due to labor problems. The policies are out-dated and the workers are unaware of the changing market scenario, recession at the market scenario, recession at the market place and competition. A few months ago we had discussed new HR policies to improve the productivity and adhere to the company's philosophy of life. May I ask when we plan to launch these?'

Sensing the tension, Advaith sought to defuse the situation. 'We need a new strategy but before designed one, we need to know what the competition is up to, to assess its strengths and strategy vis-a-vis us,' said Advaith. Taking the hint, Ananya immediately promised to survey the market and make a marketing presentation within a fortnight.

Market Survey

As promised, 15 days later Advaith and his team met to hear Ananya's presentation. Each member of the Leadership Team carried the four financial reports on AVC's performance which Rajiv had handed out in the previous meeting in addition to a SWOT report sent by Advaith's office.

An MBA from one of the IIMs, then 42-year-old Ananya had notched up nearly fifteen years of experience in the consumer electronics field. Her reputation was that of an aggressive sales person. Prior to joining AVC, she had worked with Sarex. True to her image, she began abruptly.

'Before going in to details, I must say that this exercise was an eye opener for me in many ways. My presentation Today will first examine the strengths and weakness of our competition before moving onto the question of whether our declining market share is a blip or a trend.'

'Let me begin by giving an overall picture. The Indian CTV market grew from 1.35mn units in 2001 to 5mn units in 2006, an annual impressive compound growth rate of 30%. However, the market grew only by 15% to 5.75mn units in FY06. While the percentage $ growth in 2006 is relatively poor compared to the heady growth in the previous five years, the annual increase of 0.75mn is encouraging in terms of actual numbers.

The CTV market is expected to growth by 0.5 to 1.00mn units every year. This growth has resulted in a number of players entering the market. Our top twelve competitors come from all over the world, including India. They are Samsung, Thomson, L.G., Onida, Philips, Sony. I shall take you through each of them briefly.'

Value for money: Samsung

International, a dominant player in TVs and audio products, is the market leader in the B&W TV segment and has a 23% share in CTV segment. In the audio segment, SIL stands third with a 12% market share.

The company also markets VCRs, air conditioners and other consumer electronic made by its group companies. Samsung strong market position in products like VCRs has little impact on profits, as it is merely a marketing agent.

With disposable incomes on the rise and a large replacement market consisting of B&W TV owners, the company would seem to be in an advantageous position. However, the company faces the danger of losing market share with a slowdown in the CTV industry: and a pressure on margins because of the growing dominance of the MNCs. In FY02, Samsung lost market leadership to us, and also gave way to MNCs like L.G., Sony, and Onida. I predict a sharp drop in Samsung margins.

The company however continues to have the advantage of low-priced products but has to work on the after-sale services. Samsung is likely to double its glass manufacturing capacity in order to achieve lower cost of component manufacturing.

Samsung has affected a change of strategy in the electronics business. It has abandoned its earlier position of selling merely on price and dealer schemes and seceded to give a value-for-money tag to its product portfolio. The company had acquired a host of international brands each of which will have a unique positioning. In terms of expanding its product range, we hear that it plans to focus on the fast growing 25"and 29" model.

1) Restructuring to succeed: Thomson

Thomson India is a 51% subsidiary of the global electronics giant Thomson UK and a leading player in consumer electronics and electrical lighting. The parent company recently hiked its stake in the Indian company to 74% through a buyback offer. Its performance in India has been patchy to say the least. In the past it over-zealously invested in capacity creation, and suffers from both outdated technology and high operating costs: a major pain point considering that one of the most important characteristics of the Indian market is that it is highly price sensitive. Owing to increasing competition and a low range of products in the 14" and 20721" segments, Thomson India's market share fell from 11% in FY01 to just 5% in FY06.

The company has roped in management consultants ABC and Smith & Kelvin for a major restructuring exercise of its Indian operations in order to turn its consumer electronic division profitable and help it show sustained growth! Believe some benefit from restructuring will fructify in the next two years. Some of these measures have been implemented and others are in the process of implementation.

2) Marketing blitzkrieg: L.G. Electronics

L.G. Electronic are the makers of 'L.G.' brand of televisions and the company's brand value is estimated to be Rs5 bn to Rs6 bn. Despite the raging price wars in the CTV market, L.G. has maintained its premium image. It dominates the B&W TV segment in rural markets. Internal bickering within the promoter family caused it to lose some ground in the mid-1990s but in the last two years, L.G. has recovered somewhat.

Their market share in CTVs improved from 8% in FY01 to 10% in FY06 due to totally revamped marketing strategies.

It has introduced the 'Smart eye' targeting the youth segment, and launched several fresh advertising has kept in pace with the changing market and now emphasizes the brand's technological prowess. A single company now undertakes distribution activities. Earlier, the company had demarcated the market in the North and South, with two companies marketing one brand. Apart from being cost-competitive, the strategy also ensures volume growth. To safeguard its bottom line, L.G. is attempting several cost-cutting measures in operations. We believe the promoters plan to dilute some of their equity to retire debts and fund future projects.

L.G. quality, while not quite being world-class, has enabled it to make a breakthrough on the export front. It is making inroads in the Gulf market and also exports its models to Africa, Bangladesh, Sri Lanka, and Nepal.

3) Product innovations:
ONIDA India is a 100% subsidiary of Onida Japan and has completed 10 years in India. Its key strength is technology. In 2000, it launched the first flat TV. The most interesting addition to the CTV line is the high-end digital reality creation called. DRC technology redefines industry standards by adding a new dimension of picture realism and is available in 29" and 53" Inches.

4) Banking on R&D: PHILIPS-TELEVISION has its entire marketing positioning is based on the health platform. It introduced the 'Silver Lens' technology, which senses the light levels in the room and adjusts the picture to make it more comfortable for the eyes, with an expensive advertising campaign.

Pricing is 10% above competitors, and interestingly, it has managed to establish itself both as premium brand and value for money. The company's high-end TV is expected to contribute 20% to CTV sales in 2010. It does not believe in schemes, but offers good financing options.

5) **Building capacity:** SONY India has a 7% share of the CTV market and claims to have attained the 1mn production level for CTV in India in July 2005. Rumour has it that it has invested S5mn in R&D to develop products according to the Indian consumer's tastes and preferences. Said Ananya, 'As you can see, we are up against formidable competition. Let me now turn to our performance vis-a-vis all our major competitors. Nobody in the room moved, all were aware of the importance of the upcoming slides.'

6) Switching off the slide projector's power supply, Ananya summed up the competitor survey saying, 'As you can see our competitors are gearing themselves for the mother of all battles. Given this background I would now like to take the team through our performance, marketing strategy and some of the problems that persist there.' Advaith nodded his go-ahead.

Marketing Maze

Continuing her presentation Ananya began with AVC's background. 'You will excuse me for repeating common knowledge, but I think it's important to start from the beginning. AVC is India's largest CTV manufacturer, with substantial interest in other consumer product lines such as home appliances, B&W TVs and audio equipment. Our market share in CTVs was 26% in 2006. The CTV division contributes to about 70% of the company's revenues.

Within CTVs, we have a wide range of innovative and multimedia which combines the latest in TV and computer technology. Hoover these products cater to current fads and have yet to be commercially viable.'

'Our company aims to be a global player,' she continued. 'As a part of' our global strategy we have acquired a unit in the UK which manufactures CTVs, alkaline batteries and color monitors for computers for the Europe market. In 2006, our export were approximately 6% of sales.

With disposable incomes on the rise and a large replacement market for B&W TVs, the CTV market shows great potential. However, as we all know, stiff competition within the industry continues to put pressure on our margins. Rajiv has already forwarded the key financial data to you.'

Our sales and marketing team conducted a major survey recently of consumer preferences margins and dealer schemes. These are the main observations obtained.

Consumer Preference Survey

We conducted this survey through an independent market research an independent market research agency, which found that sound quality has become far more important for today's consumers than what it was earlier. The sound output of 100 to 200 watts has now moved on to 1,000 watts. We currently provide maximum 700 watts. Providing 1,000 watts plus would mean an extra cost of 1% of the unit sales price.

Five band graphic equalizer, turbo sound, auto sound leveller, surround sound have become important influencing factors in the purchase decision. We can provide all these fractures except surround sound due to technical reasons. To meet these requirements, the time and the cost are the two elements to be considered.

Contrary to expectations, the visual brand recall lags behind GL and Flaire. This was an unexpected market finding for us.

L.G. dominates South Indian markets, Visual's home ground.

The number of dealers and exclusive showrooms for some of the major players average 6,500 average and 220 respectively.

Flat seems to be the big new craze. Sales are expected to be in the region of 150,000 units or 2.8% of the entire CTV market.

This also means an increase in the flat TV segment of 100% over last year. The players offering flat TVs are L.G., Sony, and Philips. The price range of flat TV models varies from Rs 21,000 per unit to Rs 60,000 plus. AVC's flat TV production is negligible compared to the competitors.

The high-end TV market is now integrating to a combination of what is called TV-Audio- Video Players, i.e., TVs with audio, video, computer, and Internet facilities. The price range varies from Rs 60,000 per unit to Rs 300,000 plus. The present market share is 0.01%, but is likely to move up to 10% of CTV sales by 1989.

Margin: the margins of various brands to the dealers vary from 12% to 15/%. As you can see, we have been able to control margins: we are the best in the country.

Promotional schemes: while many competitors believe in offering schemes to the consumers, we decided not to offer any schemes, since the company believed that this would discount the product. Naturally, the dealers are not happy since the margins are low and no schemes are offered.

Distribution network: we operate through a network of dealers and exclusive showrooms. The number of dealers have increased from 3,000 in 2001 to 4,500 in 2006. The number of exclusive showrooms have also increased from 40 to 110 in the corresponding period. The present distribution network is inadequate and I feel that the number of dealers and exclusive retail outlet must increase by 25% during this financial year.

What Next?

Thanking Ananya, Advaith ended the meeting. 'I appreciate the frank and the open discussion that we had today. I've always believed that the first step to solving a problem is they acknowledge that a problem exists. I now request all the heads of location and general managers to work together to formulate an action plan.'

Case Questions

1. What should be the action plan for AVC? Which areas should it focus on? All assumptions should be spelt out and justified.

2. Where exactly is AVC'S strategy stuck up at present. Do you suggest any alternative strategy please explain consequential situations?

3. Please propose an appropriate business model for AVC Ltd. based on consolidation and growth strategy for the period (5 years).

15

The Survival Instinct

A Case Study in Services Marketing

Learning Objectives

Services industries are always faced with challenges in maintaining quality of services as also the best pricing strategies for their product and services. The major requirement as corporate strategy of most the businesses in services industries is the strategic value innovation wherein with improved value the costs (price) have to be the most competitive.

The students' faculty and business executives in services industry will find this case as giving a deeper insight in to the real-life strategies in value innovation as adopted by major players not only for sustaining competitive advantage but perennially for business survival.

Case Details

Six years after running down the low-cost model, Jet Airways and Kingfisher Airlines are betting on it to keep running. On 25 August 2003 Gorur Ramaswamy Gopinath annex-Army officer who can run helicopter services on charter launched India's first low-cost airline Air Deccan. Food was not free on board and travellers had to pay for their meals. The tickets didn't carry seat numbers those who came in first got the best seats. Gopinath's unique selling proposition was rock-bottom ticket price: The fares he offered were half of the other airlines in business. Indian travellers had never seen anything like this before. The rush of passengers on Air Deccan was huge.

Rivals were smug and confident that Gopinath had committed hara-kiri. Naresh Goyal's Jet Airways publicly declared that the low-cost model

Indian Business Case Studies. Roopa Praveen, Dilip Aher, and Nilesh Anute, Oxford University Press. © ASM Group of Institutes, Pune, India 2022. DOI: 10.1093/oso/9780192869418.003.0015

was a sure recipe for disaster. Unlike Europe and the United States, India did not have separate low-cost airports with cheaper landing and parking charges which are essential to keep costs down. Cutting out the meal would indeed save money but not enough to offer such low prices and still make money.

Then two years ago in 2007, Goyal acquired full-service carrier Air Sahara for Rs.1450 crore and quickly turned it into a 'value carrier' called Jet Lite. He may not have called it a low-cost carrier. Not to be left behind in 2008 Vijay Mallya's Kingfishers Airlines which had positioned itself as a premium airline bought Gopinath's Air Deccan with the promise that it will add to it the zoning of special customer service (which meant meals on board) akin to its full-service operations. But it remained a low-cost service. The message was hard to be lost: The low-cost model was here to say.

Last fortnight the wheels of destiny turned one more time. Not content with one low-cost carrier Jet Airways announced the launch of a new all-economy no-frill service called Jet Konnect.

For all practical purposes it is another low-cost service with low-cost fares. For the new service, the company has diverted about 20% of the capacity of its full-service carrier, Jet. The service will be same as on a Jet flight, except there will be no food. As many as eight aircraft will be pressed into service under Jet Konnect for 54 flights a day on select routes.

This mind you is just the beginning. Jet Airways plans to add another aircraft to the Jet Konnect fleet by the end of May. Once this happens, a quarter of Jet's capacity will have become all-economy and no-frill. Jet Konnect will then operate no less than 68 flights a day. 'Jet Konnect has a very flexible and rapidly deployable capacity. This is being planned as a response to the customer who prefers lower fares. We will watch the loads of Jet and then think of expanding Jet Konnect further,' says Jet Airways Executive Vice President Sudheer Raghavan.

The strategy, claims Raghavan, has already started paying dividends. Revenues on the Jet Konnect routes have improved substantially, according to him. 'Our total customer carriage has gone up by 27 percent on Jet Konnect flights. Also the pace of our booking for the Jet Konnect flights after it was introduced has gone up by 1.35 times as compared to the period prior to the announcement,' adds Raghavan.

Meanwhile, Mallya's Kingfisher has quietly diverted about 10% of its full-service capacity to its low-cost arm, Kingfisher Red, which comprises the Air Deccan fleet. As a result, Kingfisher Red has now got 24 flights a day. 'On certain routes, we saw more opportunities for a low-cost model, and that is why we have decided to increase the capacity of Kingfisher Red on these routes,' says a senior executive of Kingfisher Airlines. More is on the way. Company executives say there is a plan is to convert all single-class aircraft (all economy) to Kingfisher Red.

The Game of Death

Six years after running down the low-cost model, Jet and Kingfisher are betting on the same business model for survival. The shift is serious enough for many sector experts to pronounce the death of the full-service model in the country. 'What we will see is that full carriers will connect the four or six metros where there are corporate travelers willing to pay for business class travel. For the rest of the country, there will only be the low-cost model. After all, why should travelers not go for airlines which offer 30 percent cheaper fares?' says Kapil Kaul who heads Centre for Asia Pacific Aviation in India, an international aviation consultancy.

It's an international trend All airlines across the globe are going low cost. Travellers just want to reach their destination and do not look at gourmet meals. In the US even full-service carriers don't serve meals any longer. 'That's what is happening in India now,' adds Keyur Joshi, the chief operations officer of travel country MakeMyTrip.com. in India, where most flights are completed, within the three hours, food is no longer a big draw. Cash-strapped travellers are happy with low tickets, provided the service is on time.

The axe has actually hung for quite a while over the full-service carriers. Their passenger load factor has fallen steadily for several months now, while that of the low-cost carriers has steadily gained now. To make matters worse, the economic slowdown has driven passengers en masse to the low-cost carriers. For instance, Jet's PLF of 65% in April was way below that of most other low-cost carriers including its own Jet Lite which logged PLF between 68% and 72%.

Naturally, the low-cost carriers have ramped up their share of the passenger traffic. One year ago, they accounted for 47.8% of the traffic. It has risen to over 50% now.

CAPA estimates that low cast carriers like IndiGo or Spice Jet will break even and start making cash profits by the end of the third quarter of this year (June–September 2009). In comparison, the three full-service carriers (Jet, Kingfisher, and Sate-Owned Air India) have accumulated losses of over Rs.8000 Core on their books. Profits don't seem to be anywhere in sight.

Their answer to the situation is clearly more low-cost flights. What seems to have played on the mind of the full-service carriers is that corporate travellers have begun to desert them in favour of low-cost carriers. The economic slowdown has forced companies across sectors to cut down their travel expenditure. One way out is to travel low-cost.

According to industry estimates, low-cost carriers have as result got almost 35% of their market now, up from 10% just a year ago. This, mind you, is a big market. Corporate travellers account for over 60% of all air passengers in the country.

'In spite of all the fare cuts, the full service carriers were losing their corporate customers and could do nothing to get them back. Companies like Wipro and Infosys and A whole host of Pharmaceuticals companies have given clear instructions that Junior and Middle level employees should travel only on low cost-travel,' said an executive of Delhi based low-cost carrier. Several companies have been pushing the full-service carrier for low fares.

To get this traveller back, the full-service carriers tried several gimmicks in the last few months but nothing seems to have worked. According to executive in low-cost carriers, these carriers had sold in February coupons worth Rs.300 crores to travel agents across the country at a discount price of 20%. These coupons were to be sold to corporate travellers in bulk by the travel agents but this was not good enough. The migration to the low-cost carriers has only strengthened since then.

The routes on which Jet Konnect has been launched, say sector exporters, are those on which companies have switched to low-cost travel in big way: Bangalore-Pune, Ahmedabad-Mumbai, Ahmadabad-Delhi, Hyderabad-Bangalore, and Bangalore-Chennai. Jet Airways' Strategy is thus clear the new service is expected to use the Jet lineage to wean away from the passengers from the other carriers.

Flip-Flops

Many observers of the aviation sector say that much of the problems faced by Jet and Kingfisher have been of their own making. They misread the market when the economy was slowing down and the flip-flops in their fares only went to benefit the low-cost carriers. In January, for instance all carriers cut prices by 30%, though it did not immediately fetch more passengers.

Instead of letting the low fares play for a while, a month later the full-service carriers raised their prices. 'The full-service carriers thought they could make more money if they reduced capacity and increased fares. So they did away with their low end fares what happened was that PLF fell dramatically to 50 percent and they lost more money. So the ploy of increasing fares did not work for them,' says Gopinath.

To add to the confusion, the full-service carriers dropped fares again in March to come closer to the low-cost carrier. Kingfisher announced a 65% cut in fares, which was followed by other full service low-cost carriers. The carriers also slashed their fuel surcharge by announcing all-inclusive fares of Rs.1722 and Rs.2700 on select routes. Then again in April, the full-service carriers increased the fuel surcharges by average of Rs.250. The low-cost carriers on their parts, quietly rolled back the increase which widened the gap between the two.

Can the new strategy of the full-service carriers to shift capacity to their low-cost arms work? Will they will be able to stem the shift to rival low-cost carriers? Do they have the bandwidth to drop fares? After all, costs need to be brought down drastically before full-service fares are brought down to the level of the low-cost carriers. If not, there could be a larger financial mess than ever before, says Sanjay Agarwal, the chief executive of low-cost carrier spice-Jet.

'Our costs are lower by 30%. Not serving meals will give you a saving of just 3–5%. The key saving are in better Aircraft utilization, which mean better aircraft turn around and thus higher PLF. The economics on that are very different for the full service carriers.'

Not So Easy

Spice Jet points out that 15% of the cost saving for the low carriers come from utilizing the aircraft better compared to full-service carriers sell most of their tickets on the net and do not have to spend on providing commissions to agents. In contrast, full-service carriers sell only 22–30% of their tickets online.

Others too are sceptical. 'The salary remains the same in the new low cost arm. Their cabin crew salaries are slightly higher than those of the low-cost carriers, more so on ground handling.

While Kingfisher will shift some aircraft to Kingfisher red, some of them will still have entertainments system and other frills which will increase the weight of the air craft and their by the costs,' says an executive of low-cost carriers. The low-cost carriers, to be sure, are paranoid about costs. IndiGo, for example, uses a lighter exterior paint to keep the weight of its air crafts low as possible.

The executive also points out that since Jet Konnect is part of Jet Airways, the time slots and Flights schedule will be parts of the parent airline system. In other words, its utilization of the fleet and time its aircraft spend idle on the tarmac will be too hard. 'That is why the time required to prepare air craft for its next service will remain 10 minutes higher than the low cost carrier,' says he. That could mean additional cost.

On their part, the full-service carriers think they know how to manage the numbers. They have worked out various ways to reduce cost. For instance, Jet Konnect will have lesser cabin crew. It is also increasing the number of seats from 164–175, which will bring in more revenue. Similarly, Kingfisher plans to reduce the number of cabin crew by around two per aircraft.

Jet Konnect is also looking at reducing its distribution cost which are higher than the low-cost carriers because they work on a global delivery system (an international web-based customer relationship management system). Raghavan says Jet Airways has approached GDS operators to lower the distribution costs by as much as 50% from their current levels of $6 per segment.

Raghavan also says that Jet airways can easily change the timings of the Jet Konnect flights if there is any need to improve the turnaround time without disturbing the full-service flights.

On the positive side, Jet and Kingfisher have incurred no extra cost to launch the new services. Jet Executive says that the eight Jet Konnect aircraft will have to undergo no change in configuration since they were already operating all-economy flights. No aircraft will be repainted.

Raghavan in fact says that 'much is made of the difference in costs. If we go through the major cost components of the two airline models, these are fuels, air craft maintenance costs and aircraft ownership costs. And they are no different in our model. In addition to that we fly to the same airports in the country and pay the same charges.'

So will the full services carriers onslaught to offer customers cheaper fares lead to an all-out war with the low-cost carriers? Already, the low-cost carriers are bracing up for challenge and say that fares might drop another 10–15% on select routes. Points out Ajay Singh, Director on the Spice Jet board: 'we are surely in better position to reduce fares than full service carriers.'

Case Questions

1. Is the strategy of full-service carriers to shift to low-cost segment feasible under the present economic slowdown versus government stimulants for increased spending?

2. Will the full-service carriers be able to stem the shift of PLE to low-cost carriers?

3. Do the full-service carriers have enough bandwidth to drop fares?

4. What would you recommend as a 'business model' for the other-wise sinking air services business.

16

Innovate or Perish

The Story of Perfect Fittings

Learning Objectives

Majority of the ancillary industries in each of the industry segments have their survival mostly dependent on the industry performance in the OEMS. This makes SME entrepreneur to keep a close watch on the factors which decide the fate of their customer industries more than they keep watch on their own enterprise. This keeps the businesses on tenterhooks all the while.

For a small and or medium-size company the only way to sustain and grow is to be watchful and invest in ways to reduce this dependence on their OEMS and keep on inventing and innovating on their core and competitive strengths and gradually be in lookout for opportunities to diversify and innovate to have their own unique product or services to stand on their own final customers with whom they can plan all their strategies for future sustenance and growth.

This case study takes its readers through such a situation faced by a progressive small-scale ancillary industry with their intensive search for diversification adopting and investing in new product and manufacturing technology.

Case Details

This is a story of steady development and success of 'Perfect Fittings'—a company promoted by Mr Sunil Pradhan. Starting with the conventional activity of fabrication, the promoter decided to diversify into a specialized

Indian Business Case Studies. Roopa Praveen, Dilip Aher, and Nilesh Anute, Oxford University Press. © ASM Group of Institutes, Pune, India 2022. DOI: 10.1093/oso/9780192869418.003.0016

area and with sheer determination, handwork and consistency made it a success.

Establishment of the company 'Perfect fittings' is actually an outcome of a co-incidence which came in the way of Mr Sunil Pradhan, a young Mechanical Engineer, who was running a small workshop in Pune. The workshop established by Mr Sunil's father in the early 60s in Pune, on the banks of Mutha river, was badly affected by the floods of 12 July 1962.

Mr Pradhan accepted the challenge of developing machine components for automobile manufacturers, since he realized that though it is difficult, it is definitely not impossible to venture to manufacture something new. The job, entirely different from what the unit was doing then, could be executed with little bit of imagination, technical expertise and with the help of some special purpose machinery. If successful, it will assure him continuous work orders and a size-able profit also. In the early 90s electronic and digital industry was rapidly expanding. To manufacture measuring equipment required by this industry and to introduce innovative products was a golden opportunity for the company.

Mr Pradhan asked his brother to join and help him. Mr Anil Pradhan, who had by then completed his Post Graduation and has also been trained in some companies in Germany and Japan, manufacturing similar custom-made components and C.M.C. Machines (coordinated measuring machines) which combine electronic and software technology.

Philosophy of Pradhan brothers is to share the benefits of business with the workers. In a way it is service to the society. By motivating and educating the workers in doing skilled jobs, the company is serving the society and creating new avenues for the upcoming entrepreneurs. Every industry has this onerous responsibility. Mr Pradhan believed that the present educational system-conventional education in the schools, colleges, and even in the management institutions mainly create job centric graduates. Academic knowledge lacks orientation to the industry requirements.

Now Mr Pradhan has received a very lucrative offer from one multinational company Globe Inc. who wishes to take over the entire business of 'Perfect Fittings' at a handsome premium. This situation has put Pradhan brothers in dilemma, since accepting this lucrative offer will bring them good fortune, but will lose their identity and have to compromise on their urge to help the workers and the society.

Innovation as the Right Way Out

The company has already travelled a long way. 'Perfect fittings' was established about 30 years before, to manufacture 'Quality measuring instruments'. The company started with fabrication and odd jobs and diversified and specialized in producing various measuring instruments such as gauges, equipment, measuring fixtures, and instruments to meet the industry demand. Continuous innovation, focusing on Research and Development (R&D), and manufacture of instruments at an affordable and competitive price, helped the company to make headway in many new areas. It has created an identity of its own in the field of special quality fittings required for the industry.

To recover from the losses and come over the calamities of floods. Mr Sunil Pradhan was exploring the possibility of expanding and diversifying the activity. He therefore approached a reputed automobile manufacturing company in Pune. The company offered him to manufacture certain machine components as per their specifications and drawings. Quality of the product and accuracy in measurement was crucial part of the execution. The automobile manufacturer has been importing these components and so far wanted to develop 'import substitute' for these components.

Diversification

To execute the order as per the drawing and specifications it was necessary to have some equipment to measure the accuracy. These measuring instruments were not locally available, but were required to be imported from Germany at that time. Mr Pradhan could not possibly rely on the imported instruments since the supply was uncertain. He also wanted to keep down the costs and increase the margins, which he was getting for the manufacture of these components. He therefore ventured to manufacture necessary equipment, to measure the accuracy and quality of the components manufactured by him for the automobile company. With trial and error he started manufacturing components for Oil Engine manufacturers and also for process control plants.

Innovation Pays

Within a span of five years the company acquired the necessary skill and expertise to manufacture components required for special purpose machines with the help of measuring equipment developed in-house. The profit earned by the company was invested by Mr Pradhan in developing other products to meet the demands of various specified industries.

Then came a period when the company had to face a very difficult time since there were stringent Government regulations, strict licensing policy, increasing tariff rates, and high custom duties. With determination, hard work, and the support of his qualified and competent colleagues, Mr Pradhan won over the situation and built a strong base for the company.

In the New Era

In the early 90s electronic and digital industry was rapidly expanding. To manufacture measuring equipment required by this industry and to introduce innovative products was a golden opportunity for the company.

With the liberalization and opening of the economy, new opportunities were created for the various industries in India and demand for the company's special quality measuring instruments increased. There was an overall boom in the industrial activity, new infrastructures were being created. This helped the company to increase its market reach and multiply the business activities.

By 1995 the turnover of the company crossed Rs.2 crores. But with opening of the economy and globalization, foreign companies and multinationals were creating threat to the company's area of specialization.

Mr Pradhan therefore invested major part of the profit in R&D activity to develop custom made components. As a result, with some special purpose measuring equipment the company has firm roots in the market with its selected 15–20 products. Customers also preferred purchasing from Perfect Fittings, who could assure quality and assurance as to after-sales service also.

All through, the company is striving hard to keep customer confidence and quality to establish the brand name of 'Perfect Fittings'. A proper blend of latest technology and meeting the requirements of the customers helped the company to forge ahead. The company is always on the lookout to adopt the latest and best technology available in the world.

At present 'Perfect Fittings' employs around 200 workers. With technological development, basic qualities, and expertise of workers are reducing because computer and other electronic equipment help the worker to execute his job with accuracy and speed. But this makes the workers dependent on these advanced technologies and their capacity to innovative and do creating thinking gets affected.

Mr Pradhan therefore motivates the workers to undertake innovative jobs which kept them occupied and explored their inherent skills. At the same time maintaining smooth worker-management relations, keeping the workers satisfied with proper incentives and career development opportunities are also important things to which Pradhan brothers paid proper attention. Philosophy of Pradhan brothers is to share the benefits of business with the workers. In a way it is a service to the society.

By motivating and educating the workers in doing skilled jobs, the company is serving the society and creating new avenues for upcoming entrepreneurs. Every industry has this onerous responsibility.

With the tremendous development of Information Technology sector, students are inclined to make a career in IT and related fields only. As a result there is acute shortage of technically skilled people in the field of technology and management. Pradhan brothers therefore firmly believed that there are ample opportunities to the knowledge-based workers in the industry as India is leading the way to become an important manufacturing hub in the world.

By the year 2020 India will become the centre of production in international trade. This speaks about the quality of the product which companies should manufacture. Focus on quality helps to increase customer satisfaction, control waste, reduction in cost, and market the commodity at a competitive price. As a result it helps to improve the profitability of the company.

Steady Government policies in respect of the trade and industry over the last 10 years or so has helped the industry to boost business prospects. But the attitude of bureaucrats should be friendlier towards the industry.

Mr Pradhan realized that, you tend to stagnate, if you become complacent. You should always try to adapt new technologies, think about the changes that you can introduce in your business to match with the present standards in the world. Mr Sunil Pradhan has learnt from the past experience that it is essential to monitor each and every department and activity of the manufacturing unit. With the help of advanced technology, reduction in the cost of production and commitment to give quality product to the customers at affordable price will prove the key to success.

Now Mr Pradhan has received a very lucrative offer from one multi-national company-Globe Inc. who wishes to take over the entire business of 'Perfect Fittings' at a handsome premium. The consideration is being paid for:

The Technology Transfer

Transfer of ownership rights of Mr Pradhan's R&D efforts Mr Sunil and Anil Pradhan will be appointed as VP and AVP respectively in Globle Inc. However, Globle Inc. is not ready to absorb the existing workforce which is around 180 workers, and is noncommittal to absorb even a part of them. Globe Inc. will also not continue with the social service projects-workers training started by Mr Pradhan with this offer from Globe Inc.:

1) Pradhan brothers are happy to realize the value of their efforts for the last 30 years. But are disheartened that if they approve the deal their worker-welfare, social-welfare activities may be discontinued.

2) Workers apprehend that their interest will not be protected and they may lose their jobs, they may also not get fair compensation. Project 'SAKSHAR' initiated for the benefit of worker's children may not find favour with the Globe Inc.

This situation has put Pradhan brothers in dilemma, since accepting this lucrative offer will bring them good fortune, but will lose their identity and have to compromise on their urge to help the workers and the society.

Case Questions

1. What are the essential core strengths of an entrepreneur which will help the enterprise to sustain and survive in feverishly uncertain and disruptive changes in their respective business environment?

2. What business models do you recommend for such ancillaries which while being dependent on their OEMs can be gradually prepared to establish its own product lines and customer base?

17

Indian Telecom Industry

Heading Towards a Duopoly?
A Case Study on Indian Telecom Sector Appearing to Get in to a Duopoly (Only Two Players)

Learning Objectives

Normally as faculty and students of management studies come across popular concepts such as Porters 5 Forces model for competition. It is felt that there are definite ways of competition in any industry (excepting for restricted areas like national defence, etc.) and the concepts are fairly adequate to cover possible ways to sustain in a competitive environment.

However a situation so created that the regulator himself appears to start engaging in activities which are not ensuring fair playing levels for all of the aspiring players but appear colluding with yet another major player who is able to leverage his financial strengths and nearness and loyalty to the few of the top of decision-makers even at the cost of appeasing and opposing the formidable leaders in the industry.

Perhaps this gets aggravated when new rules and laws imposed affect the other players severely and adversely rendering them totally helpless and wanting to wind up all plans of growth and survival plans altogether.

This case study is based on published details available in the print media and tries to express concerns on the apprehensive situation developing in the Indian IT sector.

When Arun Sarin, Vodafone Group Plc's India-born former CEO, was charting the British telecommunications firm's expansion into emerging markets in the mid-2000s, his home country with more than a billion potential phone users seemed a compelling choice. Sarin wasn't alone. Norway's Telenor ASA, Russia's Mobile TeleSystems PJSC, and Malaysia's Maxis Bhd were also among a slew of companies that flocked to this

Indian Business Case Studies. Roopa Praveen, Dilip Aher, and Nilesh Anute, Oxford University Press. © ASM Group of Institutes, Pune, India 2022. DOI: 10.1093/oso/9780192869418.003.0017

fast-growing market. The carriers banded with local partners, bid for air-waves and licenses, spending billions of dollars to prepare their networks.

But what once appeared to be their most-promising Asian wire-less market has turned sour. Vodafone's Indian venture with billionaire Kumar Mangalam Birla, saddled with $14 billion of debt, is said to be seeking to revamp its borrowings amid mounting losses and a tariff war. Tycoon Sunil Mittal's Bharti Airtel Ltd. is rated junk by Moody's Investors Service. In a market that had a dozen carriers two years ago, just three are left standing today—two of them, barely.

High fees, frequent policy flip-flops, endless tax demands from an un-sympathetic bureaucracy that treated carriers as cash cows have driven most of the operators aground. The industry has become the latest cau-tionary tale for investors in India, showing why despite moving up the global rankings for ease of business, the burgeoning $2.7 trillion economy with a massive consumer base remains a tough, unpredictable place for those who still dare.

The latest blow to the survivors came last week. The nation's Supreme Court, ruling on a years-long dispute, ordered several carriers to pay the government an additional $13 billion in past fees. The British firm's ven-ture, Vodafone Idea Ltd., faces a bill of $4 billion, a burden that could sink the company.

'The government is becoming greedy and extracting the maximum from them,' said Mohan Guruswamy, a former finance ministry offi-cial and now chairman of the Centre for Policy Alternatives in New Delhi. 'The whole sector is in the doldrums. This judgment will ef-fectively destroy Vodafone Idea, and what you'll have is an emerging duopoly.'

When India announced its New Telecom Policy in 1999, it said the in-dustry was of 'vital importance' with 'widespread ramifications on the entire economy', and vowed to create an 'enabling framework for the de-velopment' of telecommunications.

Record Raking

While that worked in theory, policymakers also realized that the auction of airwaves and sale of licenses could fetch billions of dollars, a revenue source key to narrowing the government's budget deficit. For instance, in a 2015 auction, India raised a record $18 billion, after getting almost $10 billion in the previous year. But in 2012, a plan to collect as much as 400 billion rupees ($7.3 billion at the then exchange rate) flopped as bidders baulked, prompting it to cut prices later.

Spectrum costs in India are among the highest in the world, according to data compiled by Analysys Mason Spectrum Tracker. The leading telecom operators in India pay the largest share of their aggregate revenue for airwaves at 7.6%, followed by Thailand at 7.3%, and Bangladesh at 7%, according to Moody's Investors Service.

Driving Up Costs

While the government set high prices, the carriers had themselves to blame too. Competition drove the operators to outbid each other at spectrum auctions, driving up their costs.

As a result, companies took on billions of dollars in debt to stay in the game even as competition among a dozen operators for a slice of the market drove down tariffs to less than a cent, weighing on their earnings. Then came Reliance Jio Infocomm Ltd. in 2016, offering free calls and cheap data on its 4G network, backed by the deep pockets of billionaire Mukesh Ambani's oil-to-petrochemicals empire. Jio's entry shook up the industry that was already hobbling.

In the past two years, two of India's larger telecom operators— Malaysian tycoon T. Ananda Krishnan's Aircel Ltd., and Anil Ambani's Reliance Communications Ltd.—went into bankruptcy. Vodafone's India unit announced its merger with Birla's Idea Cellular Ltd. in 2017 to take on Jio, but it has reported losses every quarter since.

'The Indian telecom market had three major challenges,' said Sanjay Kapoor, former CEO of Bharti Airtel's India and South Asia operations and now a director on the board of Saudi Telecom Co. 'Intense competition, high cost structure with exorbitant spectrum prices coupled with government charges and lowest average revenue per user.'

But there were other equally daunting hurdles too. Some examples of policy flip-flops here:

Tax Demand

When Vodafone entered India by acquiring Hutchison Whampoa's Indian operations in 2007, the government slapped the buyer with a tax bill of $2.2 billion. Vodafone disputed the tax and India's Supreme Court agreed that no law upheld the levy of the tax. But the then Finance Minister Pranab Mukherjee amended the tax rules retrospectively, and the carrier is still fighting the demand.

License Cancellations

In 2008, the government allocated 2G airwaves and licenses without auction. The Comptroller and Auditor General in 2010 said that method caused a presumptive loss to the government. Two years later, the Supreme Court cancelled 122 mobile-phone permits won by companies including Etisalat DB, Sistema, and Telenor.

A decade after its struggle in India, Newbury, England-based Vodafone Group has one foot out the door. CEO Nick Read said in September that the company isn't keen to plough any more money into the local venture, in which Vodafone holds about 44%. A Vodafone Group spokesman declined to comment for this story, while Idea said Thursday that it isn't aware if its British partner is looking to exit India.

Warned Lenders

Vodafone Idea has approached creditors for better terms, including a temporary halt to payments, and has warned lenders it won't be able to honour its commitments for long under current conditions, people with direct knowledge of the matter said. The company denied making such a move, but said 'all telecom operators have asked for requisite help in reducing' the financial stress. Shares of Vodafone Idea have tumbled 83% this year following a 65% slump in 2018.

Following the Supreme Court ruling on the extra fees, Bharti Airtel deferred its quarterly earnings announcement by two weeks to 14

November. Fitch Ratings said 30 October that it's placed Bharti on negative watch at BBB-, the lowest investment grade.

The court order is the 'last straw', the Cellular Operators Association of India (COAI) said last week, while Bharti and Vodafone Idea urged the government to address their concerns and mitigate their financial stress. Meanwhile, the government said this week that it is considering some relief measures. A panel of senior bureaucrats will look into steps including deferment of airwaves payments that are due by March 2021 and 2022. 'The government on its end is in a difficult position where if it lets Vodafone Idea fail, it will lead to a duopoly, which is not the healthiest market structure for any country,' said Rohan Dhamija, head of South Asia and Middle East at Analysys Mason. 'We, hence, feel that the government might step in with subtle help for the sector.'

Telecom Stress

A panel of secretaries set up to recommend relief measures for telecom companies is likely to seek legal opinion on the options, including any legislative measures needed, to alleviate the stress on the sector that was aggravated by Supreme Court order on adjusted gross revenue (AGR).

While the committee, headed by cabinet secretary Rajiv Gauba, is mulling steps such as a two-year moratorium on spectrum payments, besides reductions in the Universal Service Obligation Fund component of the licence fee, and spectrum usage charges (SUC), government officials say it may also discuss issues arising out of the SC order broadening the definition of AGR. This includes any precedent of waivers being granted on penalties and interest after a court order.

'We have to assess whether we have the right to do it (grant a waiver) or not ... we need to take a legal opinion on this,' a senior government official said. 'We also need to know whether there is any precedent, if after an apex court judgment any waiver was given.'

The court's decision to broaden the definition of AGR to include non-core items has added to the debt-ridden sector's woes as telecom companies must now pay an additional Rs 1.3 lakh crore within three months to the government towards licence fees and spectrum usage charges. Both licence fees and SUC are paid on the basis of AGR. The industry association as well as Vodafone Idea and Bharti Airtel has sought a waiver on the payment, or at least lower penalties and interest on the dues, and the government is considering their demand, among other options.

Bharti Airtel and Vodafone Idea, the two most affected operators facing combined dues worth over Rs 80,000 crore, have board meetings next week to consider their fiscal second quarter results. They are hoping for some clarity from the government on any relief before those meetings.

The officials though said it is up to the mobile phone companies to move court to seek a review of the order or seek more time to pay up the statutory dues, and that the DoT will be issuing the updated demand notices in a few weeks, which will include both licence fees and SUC dues.

Industry body COAI has sought a total waiver of the entire amount of over Rs 1.3 lakh crore, 'given the poor financial state of the sector'. If that is not possible, it has requested that the principal portion be allowed to be repaid over 10 years, with a two-year moratorium. Reliance Jio Infocomm, which has dues of just Rs 41 crore, has opposed any relief.

Loss-making Vodafone Idea, which analysts say, would face survival issues if forced to pay the entire amount, had last week said it might file a review application. Analysts said while Bharti Airtel was better placed financially, the telco too would need to curb its spending sharply, including on capex and on spectrum buys, if it needed to pay the dues in full.

JIO against Waiver of AGR Impact on Its Competitors

Reliance Jio has shot off a second letter to Telecom Minister Ravi Shankar Prasad to build pressure on the government, saying the latter does not have any legal ground to grant relief to Bharti Airtel and Vodafone Idea on payment of statutory dues based on AGR.

The Mukesh Ambani-led telco said that the incumbent operators' arguments even for waiver or lowering of interest, penalty, and interest on penalty on such dues had been dismissed by the Supreme Court in its recent order on AGR.

In its latest letter to Prasad, dated 1 November—also marked to the Cabinet Secretary, Niti Aayog CEO and secretaries in the ministries of finance, law and telecom—Jio added that the government does not have the option of going against the Supreme Court judgment to provide 'any of the relief sought' by the COAI for its 'two select members, Airtel and Vodafone Idea'. ET has seen a copy of the letter.

Industry body COAI, in a letter dated 31 October, had sought a total waiver of the entire sum of Rs 1.3 lakh crore from the government, on grounds of the poor financial state of the sector, adding that if that isn't possible, the principal portion be allowed to be repaid over 10 years, with a two-year moratorium. In an earlier letter to Prasad, following the apex court verdict, it had said that without such relief, Airtel and Voda Idea could face an unprecedented crisis that could result in a monopoly in a sector already saddled with debt of over Rs 7 lakh crore.

Jio's latest letter though comes at a time when a panel of secretaries set up to recommend relief measures for telcos is likely to seek legal opinion on options, including any legislative measures needed to alleviate stress in the industry, that was further aggravated by the apex court's order on AGR.

In its third letter on the topic in less than a week, Jio has countered COAI, by citing portions of the recent Supreme Court judgment acknowledging that 'interest and penalty have rightly been levied', and that 'there is no substance in the submission (of incumbents) that interest, penalty and interest on penalty cannot be realised', and accordingly 'find no ground to reduce the same, considering the nature of untenable objections raised on behalf of the licensees'.

A plain reading of the judgment, Jio said, shows 'the licensees have indulged in abuse of the process of court, and deliberately delayed payment of dues on frivolous and legally untenable grounds'.

The company said any cut in financial liability of licensees (read: Airtel and Voda Idea) arising from the apex court verdict would amount to 'rewarding them in initiating vexatious proceedings to delay payment of dues', adding that it would be improper 'for government to even consider any waiver of its claims' as such a proposal 'would be a loss to the public exchequer and contrary to the Supreme Court judgement'.

Jio also reiterated that both Airtel and Voda Idea have sufficient liquidity and financial strength to overcome adverse financial conditions and meet their contractual obligations, by monetising assets/investments and issuing fresh equity.

The apex court recently upheld the government's definition of AGR to include revenue from the non-core activities of telcos. Consequently, Voda Idea and Airtel may need to jointly cough up nearly Rs 81,000 crore in licence fees and SUC, with penalties and interest.

The Inside Battle to Save India's Telcos

For years, the telecom industry helped successive governments line up their coffers. Now, things have come full circle, with the government working on a relief package for the industry. While the exact nature of the relief package is still being worked out, reports suggest there are four options on the table: a reduction in license fees from the current level of 8% of AGR; a waiver of penalties and interest on past dues; a reduction in interest rates to market-linked rates; and a moratorium on dues.

Thanks to the double whammy of declining revenues and rising debt, there is the distinct possibility that Vodafone Idea Ltd may end up in bankruptcy court. The government is anxious about how this could impact competitive dynamics in the industry.

That's not all. Most of the debt of the industry is held by the government and government-owned banks. So another default will have severe implications for the government's own finances, besides pulling down an already strained banking sector.

Of course, since various other industries have also asked for relief from the government, it will need to make a strong case of why the telecom sector is being singled out for help.

The government's own finances aren't in the best of shape—the rating agency, Moody's Investors Service, cut India's credit ratings outlook to negative on Friday—and a relief package, depending on what form it takes, can impact the fiscal deficit in the near term with industry leader, Reliance Jio Info comm Ltd, which has been vociferously pointing out that taxpayer money needn't be spent on bailing out private firms which have themselves to blame for their situation. Jio, thanks to a ₹1.75 trillion equity infusion from its parent, Reliance Industries Ltd, has the least leverage in the industry.

Bharti Airtel Ltd has also managed the turmoil in the industry fairly well, thanks to regular fundraising and a recent equity infusion by its shareholders. But Vodafone Idea is precariously placed. A recent Supreme Court ruling, which confirmed a regulatory levy along with a massive penalty, has threatened the firm's existence. Its cash balance is far lower than the amount owed to the government as a result of the SC order.

But the big worry for the industry is that relief may come only in the form of a quick fix solution. What's really needed is a holistic policy approach that is not only pro-consumer, but also encourages sustainable growth for the industry. 'Telecom consumers have had it really great, with progressively declining tariffs over the past many years.'

The Pricing Factor

In the past three years, since Reliance Jio launched services, consumers have had it so good that the size of the industry has shrunk by a third. Three years ago, consumer-level spends on mobile services stood at about ₹1.8 trillion, which has now fallen to around ₹1.2 trillion, numbers collated by Kotak Institutional Equities show.

'The relief package being discussed deals primarily with the debt burden of the industry. But this wouldn't be sufficient to sustain the industry.

All it would do is kick the can down the road. The heart of the matter is that current tariffs are way below optimal levels, and the government should consider regulations on pricing if it is really interested in a three-player market,' says an analyst at a domestic institutional brokerage. Put simply, what would be the point of a moratorium of a couple of years on debt repayment if the companies seeking relief find themselves in the same situation when the moratorium ends?

But regulations related to pricing are a sticky affair, especially in an industry where the regulator has preferred forbearance over strictures on pricing. Besides, there is hardly any precedent for this in large telecom markets, and it won't be surprising if consumer interest groups rise up against the move.

And to make the matter even more complicated, there have been turf issues between Trai and the Competition Commission of India (CCI), with even Supreme Court weighing in on the matter.

On matters related to competition, the SC said CCI is the competent authority, and added that this is an area Trai is not at all equipped to deal with.

In this backdrop, the government almost faces a catch-22 situation. It can claim the SC order ties its hands-on matters such as pricing, but to opt for inaction could mean that more relief is needed to be provided in the future, or that it eventually settles for a haircut on its dues.

A Change Instance

Hints of the government's anxiety about a bankruptcy filing first came in mid-September. Out of the blue, Trai said it will review its decision to completely do away with interconnection usage charges (IUC) from 1 January 2020. Two years ago, it had cut IUC by about 57%, which resulted in huge savings for Jio and dealt a massive blow to the incumbents.

The cut in IUC to zero early next year was taken as a given by almost everyone concerned. 'The last-minute change in stance shows that the government is keen that the current market structure with three private operators continues; it wants to avoid a monopoly or a duopoly kind of situation,' said the head of research at a multinational brokerage, requesting anonymity. Vodafone Idea gets about a third of its operating profit from net IUC receipts. A review of the charge means that these receipts will continue longer than was earlier anticipated.

About a month after the decision to review IUC, the Supreme Court ruled in the government's favour on a dispute related to the calculation of AGR, and its implications for license fees and other charges levied on telcos. Along with penalties and interest on penalties, the total amount owed to the government by telcos stands at about ₹1.3 trillion, according to industry estimates.

For Vodafone Idea, the estimated outgo of about ₹40,000 crore is far in excess of its cash balance of around ₹20,000 crore. What's more, with the Supreme Court setting a three-month deadline for the payment of the dues, hardly any investors were willing to bet that the company would survive. Its shares fell to below ₹4 per share, and tellingly, stocks of banks such as State Bank of India fell sharply as well.

Most of the dues owed to the government as a result of the Supreme Court order were from firms which were already bankrupt or are now facing bankruptcy. So it isn't surprising that the government has moved relatively quickly since the SC ruling. It has set up a committee of secretaries (CoS) to suggest ways to alleviate the stress being faced by the telecom sector, news reports said.

Once Bitten, Twice Shy

Having telcos both bid for spectrum and also share a portion of their gross revenues is akin to the government having its cake and eating it too. The revenue share arrangement was part of a regime when the spectrum was administratively allocated to these firms. To continue with it in the post-auction regime amounts to a double levy of sorts.

The auction process, itself, left much to be desired. Telcos were forced to get into a bidding war for spectrum that they needed to survive. They ended up overbidding, which explains a large part of the massive debt on the books of some telcos.

With this background, some feel that a relief package will only help in undoing some of the past wrongs by the government. Besides, it's common practice for lenders to provide a moratorium on dues on the hope that a revival in the industry's fortunes will improve chances of recovery. As such, it makes sense for the government to opt for a solution that has a more lasting impact.

Talk of a floor on pricing is typically met with criticism, especially in an industry that has been a child of the country's reforms in the 1990s. But the former Trai official says that regulation on pricing in a regulated industry isn't out of order. 'Besides, if consumers have been willing to pay higher prices for nearly all goods and services as a result of inflation, what separates this industry that its tariffs only head downward,' he says.

Analysts say investors are unlikely to commit more capital unless there is clarity on the relief package and the government's stance on pricing.

The Counter View

While Vodafone Idea and Bharti Airtel's concerns are being highlighted by the COAI, Reliance Jio has a diametrically opposite view. Incidentally, while the incumbents have been reporting losses in their India mobile operations, Jio has been reporting profits, giving the impression that Vodafone Idea and Bharti Airtel's troubles are their own doing.

But, Jio's profits need to be seen in the light of its massive investments. 'Jio's return on invested capital is only around 5%, and that too after having an accounting policy that results in relatively low depreciation charges,' says the analyst at the domestic institutional brokerage.

Generating a 10% return on invested capital would require Jio's operating profit to exceed the peak historical annual Ebitda ever generated by the aggregate Indian telecom industry, analysts at Kotak Institutional Equities have calculated. If competitive pressures remain, achieving these targets will be an uphill task. What's more, Jio has made it clear that investors should see it as a digital platform rather than a mere connectivity business.

The thing with a platform business such as Tencent of China is that it operates across different telecom networks. Needless to say, the higher Jio's subscriber market share, the more likely it will be valued as a platform business, with a monopoly structure being the ideal scenario for investors.

From the government's perspective, however, there is much to worry about in such a situation.

To start with, it would need to write off large sums owed by the incumbents to the government. It also needs to worry about the impact on the banking sector. Its future revenues streams from the sector, too, can take a hit. With no competition for the auction of spectrum, it may well have to settle for a sub-optimal price for its prized asset.

While this may appear to sound like an extreme scenario, it isn't outside the realm of possibility. Sure, the government seems keen on supporting state-run telcos such as Bharat Sanchar Nigam Ltd, but hardly anyone views them as a worthy competitor in the market.

In sum, encouraging ultra-low prices may look like a pro-consumer move now, but if this results in a monopoly situation, it can quickly turn anti-consumer. To start with, it makes sense for the government to ask CCI to weigh in on the concerns about pricing and give its recommendations.

AGR impact: Vodafone Idea posts India's largest quarterly loss at Rs 50,921 crore.

VIL, in a statement, said that it has accounted for the estimated liability of Rs. 276.1 billion related to License Fee and Rs. 165.4 billion related to

Spectrum Usage Charges up to 30 September 2019 including the interest, penalty and interest thereon of Rs. 330.1 billion.

AGR impact: Airtel reports Rs 23,045 crore net loss in Q2 on provisions for dues.

The telco's total revenue, however, rose 4.7% to Rs 21,199 crore in the quarter. India revenues stood at Rs 15,361 crore, up 5.7% Y-o-Y (reported increase of 3.0%) on an underlying basis.

AGR impact: Vodafone Idea says ability to continue a going concern.

Ravinder Takkar, MD & CEO Vodafone Idea Limited, said, 'We are in active discussions with the government seeking financial relief following the recent Hon'ble Supreme Court ruling. At the same time, we remain highly focused on rapid network integration and 4G coverage and capacity expansion in our key markets.'

Airtel raises doubts over its ability to continue as 'going concern'.

While the carrier has highlighted the need for significant additional financing—which includes accessing diversified sources across markets and currencies—to pay up the demands that the telecom department may raise, it has said that there can be 'no assurance' that the company's plan will be successful.

AGR Impact: RCom posts India's second biggest loss at Rs 30,142 crore.

Reliance Communications (RCom) posted a consolidated loss of Rs 30,142 crore for the fiscal second quarter, because of provisioning of liabilities owed to the government.

The situation is dire, it's a matter of survival for everyone: Sunil Mittal on AGR

'The situation is dire—it is a matter of survival for everyone. Vodafone (Idea) is in losses, Airtel is in losses, BSNL is in losses,' Mittal said. 'We have gone through several crises but this is the most difficult time for the industry,' Mittal added. 'Lower the taxes and find ways and means to support the sector in one form or the other.'

Bharti Airtel chairman Sunil Mittal called on the government to ensure that the Indian telecom market continues to have three private carriers. He also urged the Centre and the judiciary to give 'sympathetic consideration' to the industry's appeal for relief after the Supreme Court's order on AGR left companies struggling.

Mittal also said the telecom regulator needs to urgently intervene to fix a floor price for tariffs. This, he said, is required for the average revenue per user (ARPU) to rise to Rs 200 initially, and to Rs 300 over time, for the industry to be healthy and sustainable.

'The situation is dire—it is a matter of survival for everyone. Vodafone (Idea) is in losses, Airtel is in losses, (state-owned) BSNL (Bharat Sanchar Nigam Ltd) is in losses,' Mittal said.

'We've Been Killing Each Other'

'There is one competitor who has unlimited access to finances—I wouldn't comment on that but the situation is bad,' he said soon after a meeting with Department of Telecommunications (DoT) secretary Anshu Prakash. 'We have gone through several crises but this is the most difficult time for the industry,' Mittal added.

The presence of more companies is key to consumers being well served by competition. 'It is absolutely essential that we have three (private players) plus one (state-run) players,' he said. 'Lower the taxes and find ways and means to support the sector in one form or the other.'

He urged the Supreme Court to consider Bharti's review petition with understanding. 'The honourable SC needs to look at our review petition from the point of view that there are unintended consequences and lots of other companies, including public sector, are coming into this unreasonable AGR definition, which could have never been the intention,' he said.

He was referring to the government's recent clarification that the AGR order will be applicable to all telecom licensees, which includes companies such as GAIL, RailTel, Power Grid, and others. These companies, which may have minor telecom businesses, may have to pay dues based on their entire revenue with retrospective effect.

'Our legal team were perhaps not able to persuade the honourable Supreme Court on the unreasonableness of DoT's AGR interpretation but equally, I think DoT didn't realise the unintended consequences on the larger ecosystem,' said Mittal, adding that the government should have a 'sympathetic view' towards the industry.

Mittal said his comments were in the context of statements made by both Vodafone Group CEO Nick Read and Vodafone Idea Chairman Kumar Mangalam Birla, both of whom have said in the recent past that the Indian telco will have to shut if it doesn't get any relief on AGR dues.

'It will be very self-serving for me to say that two plus one is fine. I, as a person who has watched this industry from scratch—I was the first private sector guy in telecom—so, from that point of view I think India needs three plus one,' Mittal said, referring to analysts who have said that Bharti Airtel stands to gain if Vodafone Idea collapses. He pointed out China, the world's largest market, has three and the US has four operators.

Moratorium Not Enough

The recent two-year moratorium on spectrum payments won't do much to help Vodafone Idea unless there is relief on the AGR dues. 'Otherwise, it is just deferment with interest,' Mittal said.

Vodafone Idea was left facing statutory dues of over Rs 53,000 crore, as per the telecom department's calculations, following the 24 October Supreme Court verdict that broadened the definition of AGR to include non-core items. The amount could go up, the government has said. Bharti Airtel faces over Rs 35,500 crore in additional dues comprising license fees, spectrum usage charges (SUC), interest and penalties.

Both telcos, which have filed separate review petitions, reported record losses of over Rs 50,000 crore and Rs 23,000 crore in the July–September quarter, respectively, owing to provisions for the AGR dues. The government has previously said it can't give AGR relief, unless directed to do so by the court.

License holders have to pay about 8% of AGR to DoT as fees. Telcos also need to pay 3–4% of AGR as SUC.

Fifteen telecom companies that were directly party to the case owe the government about Rs 1.47 lakh crore. The industry estimates that non-telecom companies that have telecom licenses may have to pay about Rs 2.28 lakh crore, calculated from the time they got their respective permits.

Mittal said that non-telecom companies such as GAIL, RailTel, Power Grid, and Delhi Metro will now be charged license fees even for the sale of gas or train tickets as per the wider interpretation of the apex court ruling, which shouldn't be the case.

'Ramifications were huge and therefore the review petition is in front of the honorable SC and we hope they will look into this whole thing,' he added. He said the AGR dues have added to the woes of the industry, which has been swamped by 'unprecedented competition' for over three years—since the entry of Reliance Jio in September 2016—which has hurt balance sheets and caused financial stress, triggering the exit of eight operators.

'In the quest for being in the market, we have been killing each other for three and a half years,' Mittal said. 'It is an odd situation—we need a digital ecosystem to support new age industries but equally, the industry is in a crisis'.

Rare Situation

He added that setting a floor for tariffs was essential. 'It is a rare situation where we have written to the Trai (Telecom Regulatory Authority of India), saying please regulate us, because the industry is killing itself. Tariff needs to go up, industry needs to become viable,' said Mittal. 'Also, the fact that the three of us (Airtel, Reliance Jio Infocomm and Vodafone Idea) have written to the regulator says something. First time, the COAI (Cellular Operators Association of India) has an agreement to write something.'

Last week, all three carriers, through COAI, asked the sector regulator to establish floor pricing for data services soon. Due to fierce rivalry, tariff correction was not possible voluntarily by any carrier, it said. 'My own view is India needs to be eventually at Rs 300 (ARPU), per month which means customers at low end need to pay about Rs 100 and higher end need to pay Rs 450-500, where they are consuming a lot,' he said. The government needs to lower levies to help the industry.

'You can't have telecom services being taxed like the sin tax! 30% of revenues are going in one form or the other—that must come down,' said Mittal. He urged the telecom ministry to take up issues such as lowering licence fees and SUC in some forum, given that the panel of secretaries set up to provide relief to the industry didn't take decisions on those matters.

Mittal wasn't hopeful of a refund of the Rs 36,000 crore input tax credit lying with the finance ministry, given the government's finances. 'It is our money sitting with the government and even if they cannot refund it, can they at least offset it? Rs 36,000 crore, this is sizeable sum of money, we get no interest on this but we pay interest,' said Mittal. He said however that Bharti Airtel was fighting it out in the marketplace.

'We are in a better situation—we have now decided to raise funds,' Mittal said. 'However, if you have to go in for network expansion, invest in newer technologies, bid for 5G spectrum and then build a 5G ecosystem which India deserves, then industry needs to be viable.'

Referring to the Bharti Airtel statement in the fiscal second quarter regarding concerns about viability if it couldn't raise money on its terms in the face of the AGR dues, Mittal said, 'That is an accounting standard . . . They (auditor Deloitte) called it out. It isn't my interpretation or view of the company . . . It is a standard and that is why we are in the market to raise money.'

Case Questions

1. Explain the rationality of the decision-making process adopted towards Telecom sector from long-term points of encouraging further investments by private and global players in the telecom sector.

2. How would you analyse the business environment as prevalent in the Telecom sector using standard concepts studied in business management studies?

3. Please provide a suitable business model to take care of competitive market position in the Indian telecom segment incorporating major future opportunities of spectrum availability for 5G implementation.

18

The Marriage of Convenience

A Case Study on Jet-Etihad Deal

Learning Objectives

Mergers and acquisitions have become one of the most well-known business strategies in the global economy. Increasing market share, gaining core capabilities, and accessing more capital at lower cost are results from a successful and effective merger and acquisition. However, emphasizing business strategies and financial issues is not enough. Organizations also need to focus on their human resources in mergers and acquisitions. Knowledge and knowledge management as a soft side of mergers and acquisitions play a vital role. Having a better understanding of the relationship between knowledge management and mergers and acquisitions will help the combined organization succeed in mergers and acquisitions and sustain competitive advantage.

Synopsis

Airlines business has started to lose its charm as operative expenses have become very high. Added to this competition has increased and also customers' expectations have gone up. Jet airways have tried every possible manner of survivability and when it found the going difficult started looking for partners. In this situation another airline was looking for expansion and wanted to do so in time of crisis as the valuation would be suitable the airline is Etihad. This case deals how the marriage can be a win-win situation for both of them.

Indian Business Case Studies. Roopa Praveen, Dilip Aher, and Nilesh Anute, Oxford University Press. © ASM Group of Institutes, Pune, India 2022. DOI: 10.1093/oso/9780192869418.003.0018

Case Details

Jet Airways Ltd. soared to unprecedented heights at the beginning of the current millennium. And then calamity struck in the form of the global financial meltdown of 2008 which brought many mighty corporations to their knees. Downturn in economic activity impacted Jet's performance, bringing it to the brink of failure. The management at Jet was left grappling with many operational and personnel-related challenges. It was a time for Jet to take certain tough decisions. And it did make them. With the opening up of India's aviation sector for foreign direct investment, Jet became the first Indian flier to seek foreign alliance.

Etihad airlines were started by a Royal (Amiri) Decree by Sheikh Khalifa bin Zayed Al Nahyan as a flagship carrier for the United Arab Emirates in July 2003. In a short period in 2011 they had reported a net profit of USD14 million. In 2013, Etihad reported third consecutive net profit USD 62 million up 48% from the previous year. They were looking for expansion of operations.

Analysts were quick to conclude that Etihad was very close to picking up a stake in the Mr Naresh Goyal-controlled Jet Airways. The possibility of a deal, naturally, pushed up Jet Airways share price. While no financial details of the deal have been forthcoming, experts say that the Abu Dhabi-based airlines will pick up a 24% stake in Jet Airways for over $300 million.

After all, the market last year shrank 8–10% due to high fares, and full-service carrier Kingfisher Airlines had to close its service as it was unable to face the onslaught of low-cost carriers which have grabbed over 65% of the market. Even Jet Airways, a full-service carrier, in order to maintain its market share, was impelled to revamp its operations moving nearly 60% of its domestic capacity and offer it at low fares under Jet Konnect. The only silver lining has been that airlines have temporarily cashed in on the vacuum left by Kingfisher Airlines' exit by increasing fares. But the question is how long can it last if passenger growth continues to falter?

Clearly, the sector is not out of the woods. So why is Etihad so keen to put in its money into Jet Airways, especially when the global aviation industry, too, is under a cloud? The answer is simple: Etihad wants to expand in a slowdown when valuations are low; once the market booms, it will be ready with expanded capacity. The airline has always been a pygmy compared to the big boys like Emirates and Qatar which rule the West Asian market. It has a fleet of 67 aircraft, which is nearly a third of Emirates and half of Qatar. In India, too, with less than 2% of the international market, it is a minor player compared to Emirates (over 13% share) and Qatar (over 5%). Etihad has 52 weekly flights to and from India, which is way below Emirates (185 flights) and Qatar (95 flights).

This is why Etihad has always followed a different track from the big boys—to survive and expand. The first key element of its three-pronged strategy is to go in for a bevy of codeshare agreements. Thus, Etihad has signed up such agreements with over 41 airlines across the globe (compared to only ten by Emirates), which has helped it get additional passengers on its network. Two, it has taken its relationship with these partner airlines to the next level by jointly marketing routes with them. And three, it has taken equity stakes in some of its key airline partners. It has already done so with four: 10% in Virgin Australia, 29% in air Berlin, less than 3% in Dublin-based Aer Lingus and, the latest, 40% in Air Seychelles. These alliances have, of course, paid good dividends. For instance, air Berlin generated over 300,000 additional passengers on the network of the two airlines and also revenues of over 100 million pounds.

It is a similar gain that Etihad and Jet hope will happen when they eventually tie the knot. Etihad's chief executive, James Hogan, has made no bones that Asia, particularly India and China, would be the key markets in the days to come. And he has already hinted that he will be looking at 'one or two strategic investments' which could be in Asia. He also has in-house talent to help in understanding Jet Airways, as his new CEO of Air Berlin is none other than WolfangProck-Schauer who was earlier hired by Goyal to run Jet Airways.

Jet Airways already has an ongoing relationship with Etihad: a codeshare agreement in India for seven cities and also on the Paris route. This relationship would now be strengthened as part of the airline's overall global strategy. Etihad can feed in passengers seamlessly from Abu Dhabi across the country by using Jet Airways' wide coverage of over 53 cities in India. Currently, Etihad operates in only ten cities in India. Similarly, Jet could bring in passengers from Indian cities to Abu Dhabi, from where they could travel to any destination in West Asia and Africa where Etihad has excellent connectivity.

Jet Airways can also leverage Etihad's strong presence in Europe by bringing in Indian passengers through Abu Dhabi. That is a win-win for both sides as Jet currently operates only to Brussels, Milan, and London in Europe on its own. (Through code-share agreements with Brussels Airlines and Thalys, it offers seamless connectivity to another 14 cities.) Etihad, on the other hand, has a huge network in Europe; it directly flies to over 17 destinations and through its elaborate code-share agreements with around 13 airlines offers seamless connectivity to over 88 cities. That, of course, is not the only route which could be an advantage to both the airlines. The India-North America market is one of the largest and most lucrative in terms of business. Jet Airways currently flies only to Newark and Toronto and through its code-share with United and Air Canada offers connectivity to all key markets in North America.

But Etihad can provide an alternative to Indian flyers—they can fly seamlessly from Abu Dhabi to Chicago, New York, and Washington, apart from Toronto. And through its codeshare agreement with American Airlines, it would allow Indians to fly all over the US.

Effects

The agreement could also save costs. The two airlines could leverage their clout while buying fuel; they could also leverage their bargaining power with Boeing as Etihad has just ordered 50 aircraft from the American company, the bulk of which include the Dream liners, in association with Air Berlin. Jet Airways, of course, also has a fleet that comprises mostly of Boeings aircraft and could therefore work out similar integrated deals in the future. Also, the two could pare costs by using each other's ground operations at their hubs. Of course, Etihad would also need to resolve a key problem which it will soon face: to expand its operations in India, it will require more bilateral as currently as much as 85% of the seats have been exhausted. Also the tie-up analyst say could eat into Air India's business in the Middle East as well as in the US and Europe. Analysts say that the Indian government has been chary in opening up the bilateral with Dubai as well as other West Asian states in order to protect Air India. However, a friendly Indian partner could always be of help in convincing the government, say analysts.

Conclusions

The scenario as it stands shows that it is clearly a marriage where everyone will be a winner of shares in Jet by Etihad shall be helpful for Jet as the cash striving airlines can hope to survive and get new lease of life. It depends on clearance from the authorities and how much faith is shown by both parties on each other. For survival of jobs of many employees and confidence in business to stay it is necessary for the deal to take place and clearly a marriage where everyone will be a winner to happen.

Case Questions

1. What are the circumstances that lead to the fall of the airlines which was doing extremely well?

2. Can a merger or acquisition be enough to turn around business or other factors are also important?

3. In a larger picture is survivability of airline industry in the country at stake?

19

Zomato's Tryst with Food

Learning Objectives and Key Issues

The case takes you through the journey of Zomato over a period of
11 years, and touches upon all aspects, including marketing, product development, branding, human resource, and CSR.

The outcome expected is for the student to know more about vision of
the organization and its alignment to strategic decisions in marketing,
acquisition, and human resources. The key issues that one can identify in
the case study are smoke screen decisions like reshuffling of top management, laying off employees, selling off a setup in UAE, overemphasis on
brand value, bad publicity.

Synopsis

This case takes a peek into the journey of Zomato, as it completes the one-
decade hurdle. Started in 2008, the food tech start-up has become a force
to reckon with. Zomato is known to take challenges head-on, and being
extremely proactive in their approach to counter controversies and bad
publicity. Their foray into new ventures has increased the bandwidth and
contributed to the subsequent growth of the organization. The growth
measured against the journey of a decade is truly commendable. Being
environmental conscious to add to growth opportunities, Zomato seems
to have thought of every possibility.

Indian Business Case Studies. Roopa Praveen, Dilip Aher, and Nilesh Anute, Oxford University Press. © ASM Group
of Institutes, Pune, India 2022. DOI: 10.1093/oso/9780192869418.003.0019

Case Details

Inception of Zomato

Zomato—India's most-used food directory was originally launched under the name 'Foodiebay' in 2008 at the peak of the Indian start-up boom. The founders were Deepinder Goyal and Pankaj Chaddah. Both are IIT Delhi graduates from 2005 and 2007 respectively and were working as analysts for the consulting firm Bain & Company.

The idea for Foodiebay sprang from them when after having to scrounge around for restaurant menus they finally decided to take matters into their own control. It started with a simple foundational idea—an internet directory for restaurant menus.

The idea, even before Foodiebay, was being pursued by Deepinder with another friend Prasoon Jain in Delhi NCR as a venture called Foodlet. However, Prasoon soon moved to Mumbai and left behind Foodlet as a venture too.

Soon there was a severe lack of HR and business, which kept Foodlet struggling. This is when Pankaj Chaddah stepped in to help Deepinder's idea, and they began afresh by starting Foodiebay. The graph, since then, started bolting only upwards for the company.

Deepinder describes Pankaj as a 'turning point for the company'. The team of Foodiebay was just six in number but in a short span of nine months, they became the biggest restaurant directory in the Delhi NCR region by late 2008. The service, after two years of operations, was renamed as Zomato in 2010.

Funding

Between 2010 and 2013, Zomato received its biggest funding of approximately USD 16.7 million (INR 167, 000, 00) from 'Info Edge India'. This gave them a 57.9% stake in the company. In November 2013, another lucky round of funding got a new investor to pitch in Sequoia Capital. They with Info Edge took the total sum of that round to USD 37 million.

In a fresh round a year later, Info Edge, Sequoia, and a new investor— Vy Capital raised USD 60 million for the company. The total funding of

Zomato by the beginning of 2015 was a promising USD 113 million. In 2015, along with the three initial investors, Temasek—a Singapore based investment company, also pitched in, bringing in USD 110 million for that year.

The year 2016 was a slow year for the company in terms of funding, due to bad press, cyber-attack, high operational expenses. In fact, HSBC de-valued the company to $500 million—almost half of its September 2015 value, but 2017 picked the pace up again with WhatsApp's Neeraj Arora adding to the list of investors and raising a conservative USD 20 million. This racked up the total funding of Zomato to USD 223.8 million since its founding in 2008.

With the most recent rounds of funding, things started looking peachy for the company in March 2018, especially with Alibaba's Ant Financial coming into the picture with a whopping USD 150 million.

Acquisitions and Selling

While its expansion was happening in full force, Zomato also started acquiring foreign-based companies to maximize its business. In 2013 it acquired Portuguese company Gastronauci and the Italian service Cibando. A big acquisition came in when they got a hold of the American service called NexTable which catapulted Zomato into the US market's competition.

Zomato, one of the largest food apps in India, announced that it has acquired Uber's food delivery business in India in an all-stock transac-tion, which gives Uber 9.99% ownership in Zomato. Swiggy has been the major competitor and market leader in online ordering vertical, with about 50% of the market share, with Zomato being at a distant 26%. Zomato has been eyeing to grow in the food delivery vertical; acquiring Uber eats seems to be a step closer to grow their market share.

Online restaurant guide and food ordering firm Zomato sold its UAE food delivery business to Germany-headquartered Delivery Hero Group for about USD 172 million (nearly Rs 1,220 crore). The deal with Delivery Hero means that while Delivery Hero will own the business, Zomato will continue to operate it. In addition, Delivery Hero has made an eq-uity investment of $50 million in Zomato. Surprisingly the South African investor, Delivery Hero is also the largest stakeholder in Swiggy the arch-nemesis of Zomato in the food delivery segment.

The Ups

Zomato acquired MapleOS in 2015 to expand operations and build a new customer database. This increased the functionality of Zomato by allowing it to offer online table reservations and mobile bill payment.

In 2017, the company claimed to have turned profitable in all the 24 countries that they operated in, along with rolling out a zero-commission model. This was done to give impetus to small businesses and restaurant owners across its user base. They said that their revenue grew by 81% that particular year.

In 2017, the online ordering service of Zomato also crossed the milestone of 3 million orders in one month. In February 2018, after the funding from Ant Financial Services, Zomato's evaluation reached an unprecedented USD 1.1 billion dollars. This made Zomato Media Pvt. Ltd. the newest Indian unicorn company on the block.

The Downs

- The year 2015 came in with the need of Zomato laying off 300 employees in order to curb losses, and 10% of these layoffs came to be in the US. The company expanded through its acquisition of Urban spoon in US. The model followed by Zomato was to use on-ground staff to collect menus and other information, however this was not a good fit for the USA, according to Zomato, US has been a mature market. The model of collecting menus to be put online does not work, as the menus are already available online, also the number of restaurants available in the US is 7 lakhs much higher than the 70,000 in India, hence the need to lay off the ground staff.
- Another setback in the States happened when Zomato acquired Urban spoon and rebranded the company as their own. This rebranding did not work out and the venture failed in a mammoth manner.

- The year 2016 was probably the slowest financial year for the company, and as a result, it had to roll back its operations in nine countries which included the US, UK, Chile, Canada, Brazil, Sri Lanka, Ireland, Italy, and Slovakia. To resume presence they had to go ahead with a remote management service. The downfall in 2016 may be attributed to bad press Zomato received.
- In May 2017, Zomato faced its biggest cyber-attack with a hacker breaching into 17 million user records. While the concern was overpayment and card details being accessed, the company claimed that only the names, user IDs, email addresses, usernames, and password hashes had been disclosed. The breach was resolved after communicating with the hacker who apparently just wanted to prove the security loopholes in the system.
- Zomato again had bad PR built up for it when it was just about to reach an evaluation of a billion and HSBC Capital slashed this evaluation down by 50% due to concerns surrounding Zomato's advertisement-heavy business model, growing competition in the food ordering space, and money-losing international operations (making it USD 550 million) thereby raising the company's alleged losses.
- Zomato witnessed a restaurant led push against Zomato Gold, where some restaurants abruptly 'logged out' of Gold expressing some dissatisfaction with some user policies of Gold. Proactive steps taken by Zomato to collect feedback from users and making changes based on it has turned the tables around. October 2019 turned out to be one of the best months Gold—Zomato welcomed ~110K new Gold members in India alone—which is the highest number of Gold memberships sold so far in a month.

Controversies

Zomato has maintained a very transparent brand image since its founding days which has left little room for a controversy. However, some of the biggest rumours came in when the company's top brass decided to leave in a quick succession.

In the February of 2018, co-founder, Pankaj Chaddah quit citing no specific reasons other than personal agendas. Soon after, two months later, their CBO Mukund Kulashekaran also went ahead with his departure from the company without any formal announcements or comments. Pankaj Chadda, however, still retains his stake in the organization which is roughly around 3.11%.

Along with these exits, Samir Kukreja, after a very short 8-month stint also quit his position as the president of Zomato Base, the company's cloud platform. All these exits had taken place when Zomato was on its toes to fight its main competitor Swiggy and a major position reshuffle was happening in its upper management.

The company laid off around 540 employees on from its head office in Gurugram. The company said these lay-offs were due to improvement in its technology interface across functions leading to reduction in support-related queries, thereby making several roles redundant. However, it is said that the company was still hiring people for its technology, product, and data sciences teams. Zomato has hired over 1,200 people in non-delivery teams and another 400 off-rolls positions besides creating jobs for hundreds of thousands of delivery partners.

Growth of Zomato

Zomato is a restaurant review, restaurant discovery, food delivery, and dining out transactions platform providing in-depth information for over 1.5 million restaurants across 24 countries and serves more than 70 million users every month.

Zomato has become so popular in rural India and Tier 2–3 cities, there are people who have recorded original songs on Zomato. (Song available on this link, Zomato has no contribution to this son https://www.yout ube.com/watch?v=ztNgPt-GpEk&feature=youtu.be)

The smaller diameters in the non-metro cities allow for greater orders per restaurant. Meituan, a delivery app in China services 22 million orders a day from 5 million restaurants. A rough average calculation amounts to 4.4 orders per restaurant per day.

In India, on the other hand, the capacity utilization is much more aggressive—Zomato delivers 1.3 m orders a day from 150k restaurants across India at more than 10 orders per restaurant per day.

Over the next few years, Zomato estimates food delivery business to grow to numbers that's unthinkable. Zomato is looking towards having about 200m people in India who will order food from Zomato about five times a month, with the top 20m cohort amongst these ordering more than once a day, every day.

From 50 cities in November 2018 to 500 cities in July 2019, Zomato has scaled its reach into unchartered territories like Leh, and 10 cities in Northeast, making it the first to introduce large scale food delivery (Guwahati, Nagaon, Jorhat, Agartala, Silchar, Dibrugarh, Tezpur, Shillong, Tinsukia, and Aizawl).

The company saw its revenue shoot up to $206 million in 2018–2019 from $68 million in the previous year, primarily driven by its food delivery vertical, according to the company's annual report.

It spent $500 million during FY19, a six-fold jump from the $80 million spending in the previous year. Its losses stood at about $294 million in the fiscal.

Competition

The competition in this space is going to continue to be intense, and the food delivery category is still very small compared to the overall foodservice market in India. This category will continue to grow and get built over the next couple of decades, as Food Tech organizations work hand-in-hand with restaurants and food service providers to provide better food for more people.

Initiatives

- Zomato's mission is better food for more people. In addition to food delivery, Zomato continues to focus on building dining out business—and Zomato Gold is now stronger than ever.

- Heartened by the success of its subscription service Gold, Zomato has rolled out yet another loyalty rewards programme called Zomato Piggybank. This is akin to a cashback system with 10% of the order value being credited back into a user's account as Z Coins each time they use the app to order food online.

- Zomato's venture into curated Events Like Zoma land, Literary Festivals like in Jaipur, is just a strong indication to the proactive initiatives taken by the Zoman Management to be at the top of their game.

- Hyperpure is zomatos' initiative of fresh and clean ingredient supply business for restaurants. Hyperpure is growing by leaps and bounds and Zomato couldn't be prouder of the impact that that is been made on the users, delivery partners, restaurants, farmers, and the employees. Zomato is expanding the reach of its online business-to-business (B2B) food ingredient ordering platform, Hyperpure, to 16 more cities, taking the total to 18 cities including Bengaluru and New Delhi. Zomato is set to add 20 more warehouses in India by end-2020 with an estimated investment of ₹55 crore.

- Zomato venturing into the cloud kitchen market. This underlines the huge delivery opportunity of cloud kitchens and its ability to service users heavily across tight geographies in a planned manner. Zomato is committed to developing cloud kitchens across these geographies to bridge the supply gap. These cloud kitchens will be operated by restaurant brands. Zomato kitchens are operational in 50 cities across India, with 110 kitchen hubs (either completed or under construction). In total, there are 663 kitchen units and kiosks.

- The Government took the leap with an initiative wherein the Ministry of Petroleum and Natural Gas joined forces with the Ministry of Health and Family Welfare to introduce what they called **RUCO (Repurpose Used Cooking Oil). Spearheaded by FSSAI,** RUCO targets two outcomes at the same time—ensure responsible usage and disposal of edible oil in commercial kitchens (thereby avoiding several life-threatening diseases), and reduce our country's dependence on crude oil imports by repurposing waste edible oil. Zomato has taken the initiative to be positioned to act as an enabler for Used Cooking Oil (UCO) aggregation across the country. HoReCa (Hotel/Restaurant/Café) segment consumes almost 30% of total cooking oil of the country, and Zomato is keen on leveraging their reach, supply chain and technology expertise to bring scale to this initiative. Zomato is already putting their reach (on both FBO side and the customer side) to good use by raising awareness and incentivizing responsible food habits in the industry and UCO initiative aligns well with their core mission: **better food for more people.** Zomato hopes to witness zero oil adulteration and responsible use of oil.

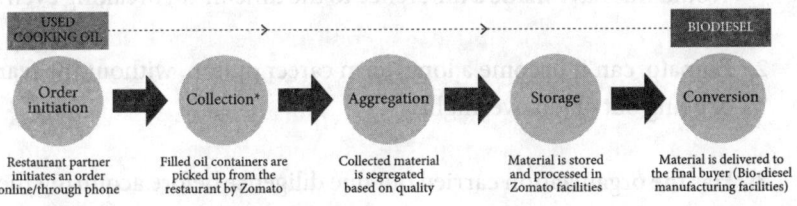

Order initiation → Collection* → Aggregation → Storage → Conversion

Order initiation	Collection*	Aggregation	Storage	Conversion
Restaurant partner initiates an order online/through phone	Filled oil containers are picked up from the restaurant by Zomato	Collected material is segregated based on quality	Material is stored and processed in Zomato facilities	Material is delivered to the final buyer (Bio-diesel manufacturing facilities)

*We pay a fair and transparent price for the waste oil collected from restaurants

Few Highs for Zomato

Zomato is on the verge of cracking its maiden profits and are all set to grow 10x in the next five years according to the Founder Deepinder Goyal. Zomato's profits have come on the back of its rapid expansion into new cities that have not only brought in more business to established outlets and 'dark kitchens' but has also created thousands of jobs.

Zomato touches 25 million customers every week, generate 0.5 million jobs directly. Zomato is still investing heavily in the food delivery business which has grown 6x in the last year 2019, and is now present in more than 500 cities.

Zomato delivers orders from around 250,000 restaurants and hundreds of 'dark kitchens' where restaurant food is cooked but no restaurant exists. Besides bringing business to restaurants and 'dark kitchens', most of which do not have their own delivery service, Zomato is also creating direct employment through riders.

The monthly income of Zomato delivery partners crossed Rs 200 crore for the first time in September 2019, with the number of delivery partners rising to 2.3 lakh against 74,000 in September 2018. The company aims to add 10,000 new jobs as a result of direct employment and contracts with Zomato.

Case Questions

1. In trying to establish the brand Zomato, have they gone overboard in spending, so much so they were devalued, leading to losses? Would this have made a difference to the timeline of breaking even?

2. Zomato, can it become a long*term career option, without the fear of being out of job overnight?

3. Has the organization carried out due diligence before acquiring the US operations? If so were the stakeholders (read customers) being misled about layoffs?

4. Is Zomato a brand that is as transparent as they claim?

20

'The Midnight Sun'

(Sol de media Noche) Entrepreneurship
Development—Western Mexico A live Case Study
(A Case Study Developed as a Joint Project between
Indian and Mexican Faculty)

Learning Objectives

What entrepreneurs can do for overall growth of the land at national level.
How product quality helps in building a long-life relationship with customers and to create and maintain brand product image. How to overcome challenges especially in respect of technology upgradation, product
development, and customer service and how to face and focus on business growth in absence of professional managers and organizational
structure. How to motivate employees and customers so that they can
be considered as core strength of an organization. How cost reduction
is helpful in increasing profit margin. How to confront the accelerated
market growth in absence of required technology. Advantages of control
over finished goods inventory.

Synopsis

Mrs Guadalupe was an enthusiastic entrepreneur, she observed business
opportunities in agricultural products viz; food products, gourmet delicacies, etc., her father and husband were the core strength of her as they
were supporting her in business ventures.

To find out the potential in manufacturing of agricultural products they jointly conducted the survey for easy availability of basic raw

Indian Business Case Studies. Roopa Praveen, Dilip Aher, and Nilesh Anute, Oxford University Press. © ASM Group
of Institutes, Pune, India 2022. DOI: 10.1093/oso/9780192869418.003.0020

material, conducive weather conditions, customers availability as a potential market and decided to explore and exploit the 'Gaudalupe valley' in Ensenada province in Baja California of Mexico for the manufacturing of food products and gourmet delicacies from horticulture, cereals, and dairy products. The family of Guadalupe anchored their entrepreneurial venture in 2011 under the trade name 'The Midnight Sun'.

Case Details

The venture was started its business initially with six main products likes:

1) Artisan bread (60% capacity utilized)
2) Preservatives (70% capacity utilized)
3) Dressings (70% capacity utilized)
4) Vegetable oils (65% capacity utilized)
5) Cheese (60% capacity utilized) and
6) Wine (85% capacity utilized)

The business was controlled by the promoters Mrs Guadlupe, her husband, and father with initial investment @ 60%, 20%, and 20%, respectively, on an initial required capital of $ 10,000.00 against infrastructure and $ 5000.00 against working capital. The business growth was steady having hiccups due to reduced entrepreneurial focus and increased competition in the market.

Mrs Guadalupe was an enthusiastic entrepreneur, being found business opportunities in agricultural products viz; food products, gourmet delicacies, etc., the family of Guadalupe (Mrs and Mr Gaudalupe and her father) anchored their entrepreneurial venture in 2011 under the trade name 'The Midnight Sun' after finding out the potential in manufacturing of agricultural products through joint survey for easy availability of basic raw material, conducive weather conditions, customers availability as a potential market. As an outcome of the survey they decided to explore and exploit the 'Gaudalupe valley' in Ensenada province in Baja California of Mexico for the manufacturing of food products and gourmet delicacies from horticulture, cereals, and dairy products.

The family of Gaudalupe was having love for the land and they considered their employees and customers as their core strength with this principle they have developed the following vision and mission of the 'The Midnight Sun'.

> **Vision:** To incorporate in each of their endeavours 'Love for the Land' and dedication to its overall growth starting from specialized in producing artisan products claiming place of pride at the national level in organic gourmet products
>
> **Mission:** To be recognized as a company in entire Mexico for its gourmet products with unbeatable taste and quality as its USP.

The organization does not employ professional managers and technical experts because of financial constrained and thus formed the organizational structure by sharing the responsibilities of total business areas amongst three of them with Mrs Gaudalupe Cortes as the Director and Mr Guadalupe and her father as in charge of the Business Operations and Employees and Customer Relationship Head respectively.

The Midnight Sun has initially employed 18 employees from Guadalupe valley who were loyal and honest in their work. Because of good employee and customer relations there was no labour union existing in an organization. The employees were divided into two categories White collar and Blue collar which were 3 and 15 in numbers and were paid @$150 per week and @$ 105 per week respectively.

Objectives

The management of 'The Midnight Sun' has set up the following short-term and long-term objectives for 5 and 10 years respectively.

1) To increase market share to 20% in first 5 years.
2) To increase the plant capacity by 10% on year-to-year basis.
3) To improve the product quality through upgradation of the process technology standardization and to expand the labour force to 50 if required for expansion activities.

4) To achieve optimization of operational costs to improve the contribution and margins of every product.

5) To improve profitability of the venture, i.e., three times in the first five years.

6) To improve the distribution channel through subsidiary stores in Ensenada City, maintain a very strong presence and appeal at the touristic and cultural attractions at Ensenada.

7) To establish restaurants at prominent locations in Mediterranean, Kumiai and Mexican Food Malls

8) To establish the brand image of the 'Midnight Sun' products and services.

'Strategy' and Business Model

'The Midnight Sun' has adopted the following strategy as a business model—'To adopt product and distribution channel as "Differentiation Competitive Strategy" with specific focus on product quality and extremely friendly and personal touch with the customers'.

Performance Achievement

'The Midnight Sun' has performed well with the help and support from their employees and customer relations and an organization succeeded to achieve better results in the initial two years itself:

   i) Year 2011 Revenues: $ 50,000.00
   ii) Year 2012 Revenues: $63,000.00 (Annual CAGR 30%)

Major Customers and Sales Market

'The Midnight Sun' with its vision and mission established the brand image and covered the direct market for selling the products. The customer ratio in terms of gender division is @ 70% women and @ 30% men in the age group of 5–65.

Domestic sale—100% (75% local-Ensenada + 25% other parts of Mexico)

Exports—100% (80% California-USA + 20% other states in USA and elsewhere in the world).

'The Midnight Sun' has achieved a great market potential of about 300,000 potential customers in Ensenada alone which is a famous tourist centre in Baja California-Mexico.

To maintain the image of an organization 'The Midnight Sun' is offering to every prospective customer who visits their store a glass of wine and a tray full of cheese and bread variety to taste and decide on purchases.

Major Competitors

Even though the 'The Midnight Sun' is doing well and has achieved faith of employees as well as customers, till fighting with following three main competitors:

1) Museoruso having its centralized stores where customers visit to buy their requirements,
2) La Manzana and
3) Quesos los Globos.

SWOT Analysis

Strength

Employees, customers' loyalty and honesty.

Weaknesses

Failure to confront the accelerated market growth
Absence of newer technology
Not having any specific plan to meet the challenges

Non-availability of human resource for employees skill-building and development

Opportunities

Fast business growth
Gaining new customers

Threats

Availability of finance with competitors
Inability to assess as to how much fresh investment is required in each of the product lines
Not having clarity as to how much organization is spending in offering free samples to its customers at the stores
Not having control on gift offered by seniors to their friends and families known to them and
Not having control on finished goods inventory
In summarization we can say that:
'The products manufactured by the organization are accepted and customers love them but the organization is not prepared to grow.'

Conclusions

'The Midnight Sun' is a family-owned organization, established in the year 2011 out of the family passion of 'Love with Land'. In absence of professional managers family has formed an organization structure amongst themselves.

The organization has always considered that its employees and customers are their strength.

Considering 'vision' and 'mission' organization is keeping its continuous focus on local recruitment, employees, and customer satisfaction, steady business growth with the support of loyalty and honesty from its employees and always trying to be at top by maintaining product quality without the hassle of major competitors.

The organization immediately needs to improve the cash flow situation and resort to cost reduction methods in the operations to maintain profit margins.

The organization is facing stagnancy in terms of increasing its production capacity, adopting newer technology and promotional activities because of financial constrained.

The organization do not have alternative to adopt an aggressive marketing strategy and become a market leader though the market for gourmet products is increasing at a faster pace calling on every player to improve supplies of quality and newer products to capture market share on priority as it does not have professional managers, newer technology, and sufficient capital.

Case Questions

1. 'The Mid Night Sun' started as a bright light in the sky of Ensenada, but very fast losing its sharpness within few years of its launch. What are the entrepreneurial pitfalls you attribute for the organization losing its sheen so fast?

2. There are many family managed small-scale enterprises which starts on a very low key but gather strength from the market response to infuse newfound zeal and initiatives to grow and expand business. In case of Mid Night Sun tremendous initiatives were exhibited by the promoters entrepreneurial family in actually shifting their residence from Tijuana to Ensenada to establish the venture and grow as fast as possible. What has gone wrong in spite of the pragmatic vision and mission the organization seems to have set up for itself?

3. Suggest remedial measures (a business model and strategy) to turn around Mid Night Sun's prospects such that it not only manages its present brand image but also grows to catch up with a leadership posture at the marketplace?